Places of Worship and Holy Sites in Europe and the Middle East

Status and Protection under National and International Law

Places of Worship and Holy Sites in Europe and the Middle East

Status and Protection under National and International Law

Elizabeta Kitanović and Patrick Roger Schnabel

(Editors)

Globethics.net CEC Series No. 7

Edition CEC at Globethics.net
Director: Prof. Dr Obiora Francis Ike. Executive Director of Globethics.net
Series Editor: Dr Jørgen S. Sørensen, General Secretary of the Conference of European Churches

Globethics.net CEC 7
Elizabeta Kitanović and Patrick Roger Schnabel (Eds.), *Places of Worship and Holy Sites in Europe and Middle East*
Geneva: Globethics.net, 2021
ISBN 978-2-88931-393-8 (online version)
ISBN 978-2-88931-394-5 (print version)
© 2021 Globethics.net with CEC

Managing Editor: Ignace Haaz
Assistant Editor: Nefti Bempong-Ahun
Language Editor: Vanessa Barreto

Globethics.net
International Secretariat
150 route de Ferney
1211 Geneva 2, Switzerland
Website:
www.globethics.net/publications
Email: *publications@globethics.net*

Conference of European Churches (CEC)
Ecumenical Centre
Rue Joseph II, 174
1000 Brussels, Belgium
Website *www.ceceurope.org*
Email: *cec@cec-kek.be*

All web links in this text have been verified as of March 2021.

TABLE OF CONTENTS

PART IV
Case Studies on Current Challenges

PREFACE

Rev. Christian Krieger,
President of the Conference of European Churches

"A people lacking a memory are a people without a future" wrote Aimé Césaire. There are places, objects, buildings, some perhaps more so than others that act as living symbols for the individual and/or collective memory. Such places, objects and buildings not only tell the story of a time that is past, but they also contribute to writing and transmitting the identity of individuals or groups, to evoking the narrative of their values and convictions, and to bearing the memory of their experiences.

Places of worship and holy sites have a particular place in this dynamic because they remind one of encounters with the sacred and focus in a special way on an experience of the divine that has been shared by others over the centuries. No-one doubts that in the Christian tradition it is the believer himself who constitutes the temple of God and the dwelling place of the Holy Spirit (1 Cor 3:16; 6:19); however, believers also bear witness to their faith by visiting certain sites. It is also true that some spiritual or theological approaches do have a more distant relationship with places, seeking to come closer to a God who is first and foremost "spirit and truth" (Jn 4:23f). Generally, however, Christianity has an attachment to places, although sometimes it may be more for the memories they evoke than because the place itself is seen as sacred. Thus, it can be understood that damaging a place of worship or a holy site is for Christians, and for believers of other faiths, a form of violence, an attack on their religious identity, as well as an assault on the right to freedom of religion or belief.

In 2020, the Christian world and the Conference of European Churches were dismayed, hurt, and somewhat angered when Turkey, in violation of the 1972 UNESCO convention on the protection of the world cultural natural heritage, transformed the museum of the Hagia Sophia into a mosque. Similar feelings now arise whenever churches are destroyed, as for example, in the armed conflict in Nagorno-Karabakh. The symbolic significance of places of worship and the wounds which result when they are damaged or alienated is clearly recognised. Such places have been specifically targeted and destroying them has become a weapon employed both in geopolitical conflicts and by totalitarian ideologies. The wounds, the memory, and the humiliation, which result from attacks on places of worship, provoke and feed ongoing disputes, create lasting prejudice, and give rise to hatred. This obviously raises the question of how to protect such places, all of which, in one way or another, represent part of the cultural heritage, not only for the followers of a particular faith but also for the whole of humanity.

Furthermore, religious illiteracy and its accompanying linguistic ignorance, which is developing in Western societies in particular, as a result of increasing secularisation and pluralisation, are also a threat to places of worship and holy sites. States and international institutions must urgently develop tools to protect this heritage - tools which will not only preserve these reminders of a bygone past, but above all guarantee free access, precisely because their use crystallises the expression of religious freedom.

As President of the Conference of European Churches I am deeply concerned that places of worship in Europe and its neighbourhood need special protection. There are various categories of issues, like violation of property rights of religious communities, access and security of worship places and holy sites, getting a licence to build a worship place etc. Examples can be found, to name but a few, in Cyprus, Kosovo (UNSCR 1244/1999), Ukraine, Syria and in the City of Jerusalem, Turkey and

Nagorno-Karabakh. In complex situations like those mentioned above, it is good that we have the UN plan of action to safeguard religious sites and their recommendations, which are a helpful tool for governments, civil society, and religious communities.

This are the reasons why this book has been published: to set out the issues surrounding this concern, to explore and study the ways for creating instruments to preserve and protect the sacred heritage and, lastly, to discuss the limitations of this approach. I would like to express my sincere thanks to the editors of this book, as well as to all those who have contributed to it. I am hoping that this publication will promote a better understanding of the existing challenges and be a significant step in the development of the aforesaid tools needed now to protect sacred sites – places which, while avowing the identity of some, at the same time speak for all humanity.

PART I

PLACES OF WORSHIP AND HOLY SITES: INTRODUCING THE SUBJECT

EDITORS' PREFACE
A QUESTION OF HUMANITY –
WHY THE PROTECTION OF RELIGIOUS
PLACES SHOULD BE
A PRIORITY IN HUMAN RIGHTS LAW

*Dr Elizabeta Kitanović, Conference of European Churches
and Rev. Dr Patrick Roger Schnabel, commissioned
by the Protestant Church in Germany (EKD)*

Religion is not conceivable without the concept of worship places and holy sites. Even the most abstract and spiritual of beliefs knows some places of particular significance and seeks spaces in which to express one self. As religion is all about the encounter between the immanent world and a transcendent reality and also about experiencing the community of the like-minded, religious communities have, over the centuries, developed a great variety of places to which they attach a specific meaning and relevance. There are places of previous divine revelation, which are sought out to partake in that experience. There are altars, where the godhead is supposed to reside or be represented. There are locations where the faithful gather in prayer and adoration and celebration. There are spaces of meditation, contemplation and tranquillity, where the person seeking inspiration, leaves the outward world behind.

Religions create places of worship, and holy sites stimulate religion. Between the two, there is constant interchange and interaction.

Therefore, the establishment, access, use and upkeep of such places and spaces is an integral part of religious life, and must, as a consequence, be regarded as inherent to religion itself. If part of religion, it must also be part of the protection, legal systems offer to the fundamental right of freedom of religion or belief. This right does not only encompass the option to have a religion, but also to practice it. Religious observance – in its manifold expressions – is the only true way to live a religious life, to be a religious person. Without the protection of private as well as public expressions of faith, the protection of religion would be hollowed out and become meaningless.

This has consequences for the protection the legal order must provide for places of worship and holy sites. Besides all else they can be – buildings, monuments, cultural heritage and so on and so forth – they are essentially expressions of religious identity and preconditions of religious life. The law, which cannot share the sensation, must share and enforce the respect every human being owes to the religious feelings of other human beings. It must protect religiously connoted places like any other form of legitimate religious observance.

Unfortunately, though, history bears witness to the fact, that humans are very quick at perceiving of the intricate and intimate relationship between people of faith and their sanctuaries when they want to inflict hurt and pain. To desecrate, even to destroy, holy places is a well-known instrument of humiliating, degrading, dispossessing, psychologically torturing people who have, for whatever reason, become enemies. As religion itself is, often too easily, being instrumentalised in conflicts and abused as a means of division, rather than unity, so are such places. In desecrating or destroying their places of worship and holy sites, the enemies are robbed of their identity and spiritual roots.

The international community is now called upon to respond, and to also perceive of this special relationship between people and holy places in a positive, constructive way by establishing a regime of protection that reflects their importance for human identity and dignity. National and international law must make it a priority to protect religious sites, as, with them, it protects not only the people currently using them, but also the memory of preceding generations that linked their life's to them and coming generations that need them for their spiritual wellbeing, their identity-building, and the reconciliation between the different faiths and beliefs existing within our pluralistic societies.

Likewise, religious communities and their leaders are called upon to immerse into their fibre the deep respect not only of their own temples, but also of all such places, regardless who worships there. This should be regarded as very simple decency, and an expression of the humanity that unites us all. Religions and beliefs must degrade themselves or let themselves be drawn into conflicts by ignoring or even condoning when worship places or holy sites of other religions become subject to aggression. Every church, every synagogue, every mosque and shrine and temple must be protected as part of the common cultural heritage of all humankind, and it must be felt by all that the malevolent destruction of any one of them hurts the essence of what being religious means for human life on God's earth.

With this in mind, the Thematic Group on Human Rights of the Conference of European Churches invited, in November 2017, representatives of CEC Member Churches as well as of sister churches from the Middle East, to learn where such a protection is still dearly missing and what means are needed to fill in this blank. We have heard very moving testimonies, was well as very insightful reflexions. We have seen a great need, but also heard of hopeful developments, in particular in international law.

This book collects the interventions of this conference, complemented by a few new perspectives needed to give a fuller, more comprehensive picture. No book can, however, give a full overview or cover all relevant aspects. It must need to be exemplary and seen as a starting point for discussion, not offering perfect suggestions for a solution to all problems raised, but setting us – the fellowship of CEC and its ecumenical and political partners – on a constructive way forward.

In this sense, with a good portion of courage to leave a lot of gaps unfilled – we offer this collection of essays as a summary of the proceedings of CEC's 2017 Cyprus conference and the discussion ensuing. As can be seen from the interventions by our host, the Orthodox Church of Cyprus, Nikosia was a very apt place for such a conference. This divided and partly occupied isle bears witness to the wounds inflected on sanctuaries and, by that, to the faithful themselves. We are grateful to have been allowed to share, for some time, in the sorrow, but also the faith and resolution of our brothers and sister to never give up hope and extend a hand for future reconciliation – and restoration.

If this book must remain incomplete in topics and perspectives covered, it must also be very clear, that it can by no means constitute a positioning of CEC in any of the individual issues raised. Views and opinions expressed in any individual article are exclusively those of the respective author and do not necessarily reflect the opinions of the editors, of the other authors represented in this book, of CEC or of its staff, governing bodies and Member Churches. The Conference of European Churches has offered, and is always ready to offer, a platform for exchange and discourse. It did so by convening the conference and it does so by publishing this book. By doing so, it does not endorse all positions and ideas that can be found in this collection but encourages a lively discussion among participants and readers.

In the hope, that this book does indeed contribute to such a public debate and consequently to positive developments regarding our common concern – a better protection for places of worship and holy sites – we commend the following to your attention.

"Towards Universal Standards of Protection" Communiqué of the Holy Sites Conference

The participants at the Ecumenical Conference 'Places of Worship and Religious Sites in Europe and the Middle East',[1] organised by the Conference of European Churches,[2] and held under the auspices of His Beatitude, Archbishop Chrysostomos II of Nova Justiniana and all Cyprus, adopt the following Communiqué:

The participants:

- Welcome recent developments[3] indicating an increased public awareness of the importance of 'places of worship' and 'holy sites' as an integral part[4] of Freedom of Religion or Belief,[5] as well as of their relevance for the common cultural heritage of humanity,

---

[1] Participants came from several EU and non-EU states in Europe, as well as from Turkey and the Middle East, for example the Holy Land and Syria.

[2] A fellowship of 115 European Churches from the Protestant, Orthodox, Anglican and Old Catholic traditions.

[3] For example, in September 2016 the International Criminal Court found a person guilty of 'the war crime of intentionally directing attacks against historic monuments and buildings dedicated to religion' in Mali; and in March 2017, the UN Security Council deplored and condemned 'the unlawful destruction of cultural heritage, inter alia destruction of religious sites and artefacts'.

[4] Cf. Article 6 (a) of the UN General Assembly's 'Declaration on the Elimination of All Forms of Intolerance and of Discrimination Based on Religion or Belief' (A/RES/36/55, 1981); the UN Human Rights Committee's 'General Comment 22', para 4).

[5] As enshrined in Article 18 of the Universal Declaration of Human Rights, in Article 18 of the International Covenant on Civil and Political Rights, and in European legal instruments such as Article 9 of the European Convention on Human Rights or Article 10 or the Charter of Fundamental Rights of the European Union.

- Are aware that such sites form an integral part of the fibre constituting individual personality and historic and cultural identity of peoples, wherefore their proper maintenance and use contributes to cohesion, whereas their desecration or destruction can cause severe trauma,
- Assert that the relevance of sites with a religious or spiritual character cannot be reduced to their historic, artistic or cultural significance, but are part of the living memory and testimony of faith,
- Repent the failure of Christians in our common history to respect and protect religious sites of other believers,
- Call on solidarity with Christians and other believers suffering from intolerance, conflict and war that eventually causes damage to such sites.
- The participants are deeply concerned that many sites of religious or spiritual, as well as those of historic and cultural significance, have, over the past decades, once again become focal points of violence and intolerance and/or suffered from hostile acts, especially but not exclusively in conflicts and wars, both from states and from third parties.

They:

- Emphasise that any building (including, *inter alia*, churches, chapels, monasteries, synagogues, temples and mosques) or site (including, *inter alia*, monuments, cemeteries, routes of pilgrimage) should be regarded as a place of worship or a holy site if:
    - A religious community can legitimately claim either the right of property or otherwise the right to use of that site for religious rites or similar expressions or manifestations of religion, individually and collectively,

- It has been specifically dedicated to such a purpose, or has been traditionally used for such a purpose over a significant period of time,
- It has a specific religious or spiritual meaning attached to it for one or more religious communities without prejudice to the property rights of others.

- Urge for a strong and effective protection of such sites in national, as well as international law from illegitimate interferences, such as the denial of access, the obstruction of religious ceremonies, damage, plundering and trafficking of artefacts, and destruction, both from a state and/or from third parties, giving special attention also to the prohibition of unlawful, disproportionate, discriminatory or otherwise unjust dispossession.
- Call on all Members of the Conference of European Churches, as well as on all other churches and communities of religion or belief in Europe and the Middle East to:
    - Seek, in the spirit of peace and reconciliation, a common understanding especially in the handling of such sites that are of religious or spiritual significance to more than one denomination or religion,
    - Engage in dialogue on how religious actors can raise political awareness together on their importance, while forestalling a politicisation of religious sites in conflicts to join in common action to defend each other's rights, with a special view on minorities.
- Expect the European Institutions and the Member States of the European Union, in cooperation with other international actors[6] to:
    - Use the upcoming 'European Year of Cultural Heritage' (2018) to increase their efforts to ensure respect

---

[6] Cf. the UN Human Rights Council resolution 6/37.

and protection for places of worship and holy sites, both in EU law and in the Common Foreign and Security Policy;

o Work towards a comprehensive international regime of legal protection, building on a better understanding of the fundamental right to Freedom of Religion or Belief, and include a common definition of such places and sites, as well as legal remedies to ensure proper implementation. In particular, religious communities must be able to acquire or build, own and administer, maintain or restore access and use such places.

PLACES OF WORSHIP
AND RELIGIOUS MONUMENTS
IN EUROPE AND THE MIDDLE EAST: STATUS AND PROTECTION
UNDER NATIONAL AND INTERNATIONAL
LAW - OPENING ADDRESS

His Beatitude Archbishop Chrysostomos II of Nova Justiniana and All Cyprus

Today's conference, organised by the Conference of European Churches on the 'Places of Worship and Religious Monuments in Europe and the Middle East: Status and Protection Under National and International Law', takes place at a very difficult and crucial time for the sensitive region of the Eastern Mediterranean, the cradle of civilisation from which 'the light of knowledge' arose and 'grace and truth came into being through Jesus Christ' (John 1, 17).

At this turbulent time and, indeed, in this area of the world, which is being particularly sorely tested, we, as politicians and religious leaders, are being called upon to carry out our role and make an active contribution by creating a better and happier world in our region, one without wars and bloodshed. Moreover, in a spirit of goodwill and mutual understanding, we need to study the problems that we are facing, take decisions, come up with answers and resolve them successfully. The presence of all of you here today underlines, and is testament to, the great significance of today's conference.

Developments in our region are unfolding rapidly and we, as spiritual leaders, cannot remain mere observers of everything that is happening around us or simply follow events. Christians have lived in the Middle

East since antiquity and any attempt to expel or force them to leave must be viewed as unfair and unjustified. After all, the Christian element has adapted to, and coexisted in peace and harmony with other religious elements that have arisen throughout the centuries.

Unfortunately, however, the prevalence in recent times of extreme fundamentalist elements in the region has placed the very existence of Christians in their ancient lands in immediate danger. We are witnesses, on a daily basis, to attacks on places of Christian worship, the murder of innocent people, abductions, violence and barbarity against Christian property and violations of Christians' most basic human rights. It is in such circumstances that Christians are being forced out and thousands have already abandoned their ancient homelands and sought shelter as refugees in various places offering them greater safety and security.

My country, Cyprus, was once a place of religious pluralism, in which 80% of the population were Greek Cypriot Orthodox Christians, 18% Turkish Cypriot Muslims and the remaining 2% Maronites, Armenians and Latins. Until 1974, when the Turkish invasion took place, they all lived together in peace and friendship in their mixed villages and towns, each free to worship their own God. There were never any religious disputes, conflicts or troubles. The situation has not changed and remains the same today in the government-controlled areas of the Republic.

However, we regret to note that, unfortunately, in the Turkish occupied northern part of the island, religious freedoms have not been respected or implemented for the past forty-three years. Moreover, the Turkish invasion forces and the illegal regime, supported by Turkey, have undertaken an unprecedented brutal and cruel effort to destroy and loot our religious sites and monuments, our churches and monasteries, our altars and hearths, and even our cemeteries – essentially everything that bears witness to the existence and presence of the Christian population in the northern area of Cyprus.

For the Church of Cyprus, a longstanding issue has been that of respect for the obvious right to access, use, operate, restore and conserve more than 500 churches that have been desecrated and abandoned by the ravages of time. Of great importance to us, furthermore, are other sites linked to the places of worship, such as cemeteries. All those in the occupied areas have been looted and destroyed.

With these thoughts in mind, we warmly congratulate the Conference of European Churches, as well as the Representation of the Church of Cyprus to the European Union, for the organisation of this conference in our country and we thank them for their kind invitation to address these few words to you.

PART II

PLACES OF WORSHIP AND HOLY SITES:
DEFINING THE SUBJECT

Theological Reflections

1

FAITH SEEKS SPACE:
How We Relate To Places of Worship
(A Protestant Perspective)

*Rev. Dr Clemens W. Bethge, Protestant Church
Berlin-Brandenburg-Upper Lusatia*

There are many different ways to look at the concept of sacred space and reflect on church buildings. However, it is most likely that, when speaking of places of worship and holy sites, a person's own experiences of sacred space will play a vital role in how that person conceives of sacred spaces and how they make sense of it.[1] Reflections on this subject cannot help but be related to personal experiences, places visited, buildings that have had an impact and influenced beliefs and faith. The church of my childhood comes to mind, a beautiful Neo-Gothic church in Southern Germany, a great space, flooded with light. I remember the church services attended there with my parents and brothers. The hymns we sang still resonate with me. I picture the minister and how we gathered for the Lord's Supper around the altar. It has become a part of me and my faith.

Most believers (and, in fact, non-believers) will have their own personal experiences with places of worship and holy sites, which in turn will impact their faith. One thing is certain: all experiences are inextri-

---

[1] Cf. Clemens W. Bethge: Kirchenraum. Eine raumtheoretische Konzeptualisierung der Wirkungsästhetik, (Praktische Theologie heute 140), Stuttgart 2015.

cably linked to the concept of space and place. There is no experience that is separable from space. All experiences have taken *place* (in the proper sense of the word).

This paper will focus on sacred space, on places of worship and holy sites in three stages. Firstly, the two antagonistic types of places of worship and holy sites that have been characteristic in Christianity. Secondly, what it means when we talk about places and sites, in this case mainly referring to churches and church buildings. In the past, places of worship and holy sites were not at the centre of theological thinking. They were addressed as a place, as a site, as a building with history, and rarely conceived of as a space. Recently this has been changing, with that perspective expanding into the theory of space and a spatial perspective. The third part will address places of worship and holy sites as spaces.

1. Places of Worship and Holy Sites – a Basic Typology

In Christianity and, in fact, in all the world's religions, there are two forms of places of worship and holy sites: the temple-type or *domus dei,* and the meeting-house type or *domus ecclesiae.*[2] Temple-type refers to holy sites that are considered as the dwelling of God, a place where the divine and human meet. In contrast, the meetinghouse type is a meeting point of a community for religious purposes, a place where a community gathers for worship. Both mirror the different attitudes within the history of Christianity and theology and underlying each is the tension between an immanent presence of God and his transcendent deity.

We can see this tension at work between those two types in the different ways the temple is described in the Old Testament. The first Book of Kings describes at length how Solomon builds the temple (1 Kings 5:1-9:9). And Solomon addresses God: 'I have indeed built a magnifi-

---

[2] Those two concepts have been described in a phenomenological approach by Harold W. Turner: From Temple to Meeting House. The Phenomenology and Theology of Places of Worship, (Religion and Society 16), Den Haag 1979

cent temple for you [God], a place for you to dwell forever' (1 Kings 8:13). Later, however, Solomon is more reflective. In his prayer of dedication, he asks, 'But will God really dwell on earth? The heavens, even the highest heaven, cannot contain you. How much less this temple I have built!' (1 Kings 8:27). In Ancient Israel, two groups of people stand for each of those two concepts: the priests and the prophets, and two types of buildings: the temple and the synagogue. The sceptical view taken by the prophets culminates in early Christianity, in the New Testament and with the church fathers (e.g. Saint Justin, Clement of Alexandria). Saint Paul puts it in plain terms in 1 Corinthians 3:16, 'Don't you know that you yourselves are God's temple and that God's Spirit dwells in your midst?'

At first, Christians seem to have used temple and synagogue buildings naturally. As distance grew between their old faiths and new, they met in private houses. Christianity took a long path from its house churches via the Constantine basilica churches to medieval cathedrals and, now, to this tremendous variety of places of worship and holy sites and church buildings all over the world.

Both lines of tradition, the temple-type and the meeting house-type, can be followed throughout history. In all places of worship and all holy sites this tension is at work: the embodiment of the transcendence of God in a confined space and the representation of something that is in fact un-representable. Every building, every place, every site incorporates this tension, this ambiguity between transcendence and immanence.

2. Places of Worship and Holy Sites – Places in Time

Today, what is characteristic for a place of worship, for a holy site? A place of worship, a holy site, is the result of the influences that give them their individual shape when being erected and over time throughout their use. All those influences are inscribed like a text, meaning that all those influences have become elements of that place. They have been incorporated deep within its structure. To some extent, they can even be deciphered on its surface. History has left its mark on places of worship and holy sites and continues to do so. Over time, they have become material and physical testimonies of their era. They reflect history and histories, including the scars of conflict.

Take the church of our childhoods. Many people have had family celebrations here: weddings, baptisms, confirmations. Many people met one another and met God. This is where they mourned their deceased loved ones and where they sought solace. Church services have been held here and many a great festivity, and all this is visible. How many children have been baptised at the baptismal font? The cenotaphs, other memorials, the prayers left on the notice board, the comments in the visitor book, the lighted candle and the well-trodden stone steps leading up to the pulpit, all represent history and histories. When a minister climbs the steps to preach,, he can feel all those before him who preached the word of God from that spot. The atmosphere of the place, the life that has taken place here, the life of individuals and of the many, all these can be felt. The events that have taken place: historical, political events, the stories of people's lives and of society, are all imprinted on this place. This makes for the inherent communal value of places of worship and holy sites and what makes them such a valuable religious and cultural heritage, not only for a religious community but for society as a whole.

These places are not museums. In theological debate, this criticism is frequently offered when a place of worship is portrayed as a series of personal histories. The point is that they connect people with the past and with what people have become, what they are today. They make past things present, which is the basic mode of faith: remembering what God has done. In remembering, the past is brought into the present and this can be described as the religious dimension of places of worship. In many ways, they depict Christian topics. Every holy site expresses how people have seen themselves and their role in this world in the light of God. In this way, these places and sites transcend this world. Places of worship and holy sites bear witness to the belief that there is more than just the visible, and that every place of worship and every holy site is a sign of God's love and of hope for this world.

This may be seen as a deeply religious way of understanding places of worship or holy sites. It is a matter of faith and whether these places of worship are considered as a sign of God's love and of hope for this world. That is a specific response, a specific interpretation of the experience that people make within a space.

3. Places of Worship and Holy Sites and Us: Space

Places and sites, as such, offer a materialised history, stories and Christian topics, 'theology in stone', as it were.[3] There is one vital element missing from the equation, one crucial ingredient: the people who go to these places and worship, the people who use them, the people who experience this space as holy. The place and the site can be called a 'potential structure', which is to be 'concretized' by the user.[4] Space is dynamic. It unfolds gradually when being perceived physically with all the senses and when a person responds to the potential offered by a place or a site. If the architectural structure is one vital part of what space is, then the response to it is the second vital part of space. How a place or site is concretized at a given time depends on the individual's response. In other words, the meaning attributed to it, in whether it is

---

[3] Cf. Richard Kieckhefer: Theology in Stone. Church Architecture from Byzantium to Berkeley, Oxford/New York 2004.

[4] Cf. Wolfgang Iser: The Act of Reading. A Theory of Aesthetic Response, Baltimore 1978, esp. pp. 21 and 171ff. Here, Iser cites Roman Ingarden and his concept of the concretization of literary works.

considered a holy site or sacred space, is the result of an individual's personal response to time spent within it.

There are indeed many ways to make sense of a place or site. As for places of worship and holy sites, one vital use is liturgy and worship. It is vital to the basic mode of faith to remember what God has done and to make past things present. For when there is worship, when liturgy is celebrated, the past things are made present and the belief is that Jesus Christ is present through the Holy Spirit. This use is what could be described as 'spiritual respiration' of a place. When it ends, it dies.

There is, of course, a variety of uses other than the liturgical. Today, people make religiously connoted experiences with places of worship and holy sites in varying forms and various contexts: spiritual, aesthetic, political and even just touristic. This is something particularly important when talking about places of worship and holy sites in the 21st century. They are not only *domūs ecclesiae* or community meetinghouses. They do not belong to the congregation, nor are they the property of the church (even if they are in a legal sense). They never have been, they have always had a wider appeal, as can be seen from the scale of history and the stories of lives and society that are imprinted on a place or site. Places of worship and holy sites are also buildings for individual people to experience, as well as for religious communities. These spaces are important components of religious life and of the free exercise of religion. And, of course, accessibility is key.

Places of worship and holy sites appeal to many people, whether it is the space, the atmosphere, all that affects the entire body and all the senses. At the same time, it transcends all presence. Take the church of our childhoods: the slightly damp, cold smell of the stone pillars, the echo of our footsteps down the aisle, the statues and the symbols and how the light shone through the stained-glass windows. The feeling of the wide space broadened and deepened our existence. This is the potential that places of worship and holy sites offer. They must be protected at all cost.

2

THE WHOLE IS GREATER THAN THE SUM OF ITS PARTS: APPROACHING A THEOLOGICAL UNDERSTANDING OF THE HOLY LAND AND THE HOLY CITY OF JERUSALEM

His Beatitude Patriarch Theophilos III of Jerusalem and all Palestine

The matter before us is one of the utmost seriousness. The invitation to this conference outlined, in a concise and clear way, why the status and protection of holy sites are of such urgent importance.

Holy sites are, of course, first and foremost holy to the particular religious tradition of which they are a witness. They are primarily places of worship and spiritual refreshment, and they are often the destination of pilgrims, as well as frequent, regular places of worship for local religious communities.

But, as this conference recognises, the significance and importance of holy sites are broader. To quote from a document preliminary to this gathering, 'holy places can be sources of tensions which can affect peaceful coexistence instead of fostering social plurality and diversity'. This conference recognises that holy places have a wider significance and are 'not only the concern of believers'. [1]

---

[1] Invitation to the CEC 2017 Cyprus conference, see annex.

Fundamentally, this conference acknowledges that the international community must understand and support the fact that there is 'a particular right to manage holy sites, a right to own them, to gather there for religious purposes, and to perform religious ceremonies…we are speaking about the living heritage of holy places'.

We cannot overstate the crucial nature of these primary points in any discussion about holy places, and we wish to elaborate on them by considering Jerusalem as a holy site.

When we think of Jerusalem, we often think of the city as a place of holy sites, and this is true. Contained within the Old City are scores of holy sites and, in the immediate vicinity, there are many more. But today we wish to think of Jerusalem as a holy site in and of itself. We believe that this perspective will give us a singular insight into the subject before us.

There are many holy sites around the world, and many holy places that are the object of veneration to more than one religious group. But there is no other place on earth like Jerusalem. Jerusalem is unique in so many respects and this is well enough known that we do not need to enumerate those details here.

Yet we do wish to put forward the concept of Jerusalem as a holy site in and of itself, and not only as a geographical area has that contained holy sites.

What is the significance of this position?

First, to say that the city itself is a holy site is to say something about its fundamental religious and spiritual identity. While there are or have been other cities and towns that have taken the adjective *holy* to themselves – one thinks of Constantinople and Rome, for example – no other city has had an identity similar to Jerusalem. And no other city has borne this kind of identity for anywhere near as long as Jerusalem.

When we consider that Jerusalem is holy not to one but to three of the world's major religious traditions, we find that Jerusalem sets itself apart in every respect.

But as we know, holiness is not just about geography. It is also about a less tangible but just as compelling landscape – the landscape of the divine-human encounter.

The Holy Land is the only place on earth where, so the Abrahamic traditions affirm, God has communicated with humanity in clear and direct ways, and Jerusalem has been at the centre of this divine-human activity for millennia.

This is the only place on earth that has been visited by all the prophets, that has been nurtured by their blood, and that has been nurtured by the blood of the Righteous One, Jesus Christ.

This is the place on earth that gives hope to countless millions of people, near and far, who understand deep within their souls that Jerusalem is not simply an earthly city but a promise of the peace and unity of all humankind. There is no more compelling evidence of this than in the thousands of pilgrims who flock to Jerusalem every month and who long to drink from the spiritual springs of the water of life that Jerusalem provides.

We cannot deny that Jerusalem is a contested holy site. Human failure and human sinfulness scar Jerusalem as much as they scar every other endeavour. But this is itself also evidence of the fundamental identity of Jerusalem as a holy site, for in these difficulties the eye of faith sees the force of evil that attempts to destroy the power that Jerusalem holds in its vocation as the true spiritual home of all humanity.

We must also always remember a great truth about holy places. While it is clear that holy places fall under the care and protection of particular religious groups, and for administrative purposes in our contemporary world we speak of *ownership* and the care and guardianship of them, it is crucial, from a spiritual perspective, that we understand that we do not possess holy places; they possess us. They embrace us in the mystery of the divine-human encounter. While divine providence has given the holy places to our care, we give ourselves to these holy places so that we may be true witnesses, true servants of the martyria of the holy places.

All these observations mean that any undermining of the true nature of holy places is a very serious matter indeed. This conference is considering a range of important questions. Here we would like to give examples of how the fundamental nature of Jerusalem as a holy site is being undermined.

For generations the sacred character of the Holy Land has been protected by the status quo, which is recognised by both religious and civil authorities and the international community as protecting and guaranteeing the rights and privileges of the churches, especially with respect to the holy sites and to other religious activity. The provisions of the status quo have been upheld carefully by successive civil authorities in our region.

Over the last several months, we have seen a new level of threat to the stability of our multi-ethnic, multi-cultural, multi-religious society of which our holy sites are concrete evidence.

Over the last few years, there has been a marked and disturbing increase in so-called 'price tag hate crimes', which are directed in many cases to the vandalism and desecration of holy places. While these acts have been condemned by all, including governments, they continue, and effective ways of preventing them and punishing the perpetrators are still to be found.

More threatening to the status quo and the rights of religious minorities is a proposed bill that is circulating in the Knesset and that would, if passed, severely intrude on the rights of the churches over their properties. Whether this bill has a chance of being passed is not the point; the mere fact that it has gained the signatures of one third of the members of the Knesset and is being discussed at all is a new level of threat to the diversity of our society and the manner in which holy places have been managed and cared for.

Most significant and worrying, however, are the underhanded actions of radical settler groups who, in the majority of cases, acquire property in Jerusalem's Old City and elsewhere, utilizing illegitimate methods of coercion and undue authority. The most recent issue concerns the properties owned by the Patriarchate and known as the 'I at Jaffa Gate' case, in which a radical settler group has for many years been attempting to take over properties in the Christian Quarter of the Old City and thereby diminish the Christian presence in Serti-salem. They claim to have acquired these properties through what we consider *illegitimate agreements that lack due authority*. Crucially negative was the fact that the District Court handed down a wrongful judgment in favour of the settler group. This judgment was in our view incorrect with respect to matters of law and we are contesting it in the High Court and bringing the matter to the international community for support.

The movement of these radical settler groups must be curbed and controlled and their intimidating tactics to rid Jerusalem of non-Jews must be resisted to preserve the crucial multi-faith tapestry of Jerusalem.

When we understand Jerusalem itself as a holy site, and not just the place where holy sites are found, these threats become even more serious. And these incursions into traditional rights and protections of the Church in the Holy Land affect not just one religious group but all.

As we consider in this conference what we all understand to be the 'living heritage of holy places', the issues that are currently before us in Jerusalem are of pressing concern to us all.

3

MORE THAN WOOD AND STONES: HOW THE DESTRUCTION OF HOLY SITES AFFECTS RELIGIOUS IDENTITY

Rev. Dr Göran Gunner, Uniting Church in Sweden

Cultural heritage is a concept that seeks to capture the value of what previous generations created and which continues to be significant to future generations. Cultural heritage can refer to buildings, monuments, cemeteries, tombs, objects, symbols and contexts that have given great value to the identity of an individual or great value to a local region, to a nation, or even to the universal heritage of humanity. The norm is that any heritage is maintained, protected and thus preserved. Yet, what happens to a religious cultural heritage which has shaped the religious identity of the individual and groups of individuals when that heritage is threatened by dark shadows in the form of violence and destruction? What happens when holy sites or objects, older or newer, are *de facto* destroyed or eliminated? Other threats may be that a cultural heritage is exploited for economic gain or that buildings for religious practice become a battlefield between different ideologies, religious views or extreme political beliefs.

The reflections here will focus on the importance of holy sites for human beings. They could be in relation to destroyed Muslim mosques, Jewish synagogues, Buddhist monuments, Hindu temples, Christian cathedrals or churches, sacred sites for indigenous peoples, in a historical situation or a present-day situation, but most will centre on holy Christian sites.

Sunday worship had just finished in Lahore on the morning of 22 September 2013 when people started talking into their mobiles and amongst themselves. The message quickly became clear and brutal. A twin suicide bomb attack had taken place in All Saints Cathedral in Peshawar in Pakistan. The result was devastating, with 127 dead and at least 170 injured[1], among them many children. An elderly minister said afterwards, 'I performed the baptism, the wedding and now the funeral'. The partially destroyed building could be restored but what of the survivors? Belonging to a targeted minority, the faithful worshippers had built their identities and lives through the church. How would it be possible to continue with church life after this ruthless attack? Would the surviving individuals be so traumatized that their *entire worlds* would be forever damaged? In this case, the building could be restored but what happens when all trace of the holy site is gone or when no worshippers remain? As was the case with the holy sites after the partition of Cyprus or with churches during the rule of Soviet Union and just as occurred with churches and monasteries destroyed under the so-called Islamic State (Daesh) in Syria and Iraq.

This can also apply following agreed upon decisions on the dismantling or sale of a church. It may greatly impact the faithful who look upon the building as integral to their identity. For example, since 2000 in Sweden, all church buildings belonging to the Church of Sweden are lawfully declared to belong to Swedish national cultural heritage. They should be preserved as a heritage open and common to all people.

In Maglarp, a small village in the countryside of southern Sweden, the congregation had two church buildings. The old church was built around 1200 and was well-preserved with main parts dating from the

---

[1] The number may differ in different sources.

original construction. A new Maglarp church was built in 1909 and the old one was taken out of service and then reopened in 1971. Regular worship returned to the old church, with the last worship in the new church taking place in 1976. Years passed and the congregation could not afford the upkeep of both churches and was forced to demolish one. It was headline news across Sweden. After removing the new church in 2007, many congregational residents regretted the decision and expressed warm feelings for the church – it had been so important, had been a landmark for 100 years, was part of their identity with memories of baptisms, funerals and weddings. When the church was torn down, many people wanted a tangible keepsake of the church, even if just a stone.[2]

What happens if a church with a cultural heritage is wilfully destroyed through bad intentions and against the will of the believers and the congregation, or if the members of the congregation are forced to move away or flee, sometimes to save their lives? Religious buildings like churches are, in some contexts, particularly vulnerable to a political game. They can be destroyed or damaged as a manifestation of a victory of a conflict, to establish dominance or to oppress and terrorize a minority faith group. In extreme cases, it is done to eradicate both individuals and religious symbols, in the form of buildings, which give individuals their identity. The acts performed are thus a drastic way of trying to rewrite history and obliterate religious and cultural treasures.

In some instances, a few survivors may try to uphold the memory of a holy site. Take this elderly woman from a small village in Anatolia in present day eastern Turkey.[3]

---

[2] Davidsson Bremborg, Anna, 'När en kyrka rivits. En enkätundersökning om Maglarps nya kyrka', in: Svenskt gudstjänstliv 84, 2009, 60-84.

[3] See also: Back to Ararat, Documentary film By PeA Holmquist, in cooperation with Göran Gunner, Jim Downing, Suzanne Khardalian and Göran Gunér. First shown on Swedish Television (TV 2), 5 December 1989.

Elderly lady from Anatolia © Göran Gunner

The 92-year old lady became a refugee in her own country at the age of twenty. The family was left alone when the roots of the village were torn away but the narrative lives on in the family, the only Christian household remaining from several 1000 inhabitants once present in 1915. 'They hung a sign on our door saying that this house should remain. We continued to dwell here when everyone else had to leave, were deported. They were all thrown into wells, killed with knives, swords and axes.' Each week, the lady went to the lingering stones of the once-huge church to light a candle, until the remaining stones were covered with candle wax and candle stubs. Year on year, decade by decade, she went to uphold the memory of her holy site, despite everyone being gone. It was still part of her spiritual identity and her place of worship.

A trip to old Armenia (Anatolia) to investigate what had come of more than 2000 Armenian churches and monasteries that existed in 1915 gave discouraging results. Other than a few churches still in use, for example in Mardin and Diyarbakir, and a few remaining historical monuments, as in the ruined city of Ani and the church on the island Aghdamar,[4] other churches and monasteries had either been completely wiped out or were in ruins or were nothing more than few stones.[5]

Ktuts monastery, on an island in the Lake Van © Göran Gunner

Churches and monasteries should have been some of the safest places to seek refuge but that was not the case. The stories of the past continue to live, however, in stories told by survivors and eyewitnesses, as they are passed on from generation to generation. Memories of what happened are meaningful to the children and grandchildren of survivors, as well as to the rest of the world trying to grasp the twentieth century's

---

[4] After 1915, the medieval Armenian Apostolic Cathedral of the Holy Cross was exposed to vandalism and even faced an order of destruction. In 2005, Turkey started the renovation of the building but considered it to be a museum. Defne Över discusses how the building is treated today in Cultural Tourism and Complex Histories. The Armenian Akhtamar Church, the Turkish State and National Identity. New York: Springer Science, 2016.

[5] William Dalrymple made a trip through parts of the geographical Byzantium, recording a fascinating travel account of what he found remaining of churches and monasteries. Dalrymple, William, From the Holy Mountain. A Journey in the Shadow of Byzantium. London: Harper Press, 1997.

first genocide. It enters a common narrative strengthening the identity of today's world.

It may be argued that the restoring of suffering human beings who have been violated against is at the heart of the Christian message. The identity of the church, the Body of Christ, is dependent on the ability to deal with realities of violations, abuses, massacres, and crimes against humanity. Theologian Miroslav Volf has lived through compulsory military service in former Yugoslavia. In his book, *The End of Memory: Remembering Rightly in a Violent World*, he deals with wrongdoing suffered, the memory of abuse and how these are recalled and what happens to the memory of those violations. He remarks that when we hold on to the wrongs, we defer to the wishes of the evildoers, as well as paying too much respect to evil itself.

'We will not "forget" to be able to rejoice; we will rejoice and therefore let those memories slip out of our minds! The reason for our non-remembrance of wrongs will be the same as their cause: our minds will be wrapped in the goodness of God and in the goodness of God's new world and the memories of wrongs will wither away like plants without water.'[6]

It seems that, as the years pass, a collective memory appears for the offspring of survivors, the details of individual personal experiences are intertwined into an unforgettable narrative. This happened to families, to villages, to peoples, to nations.

There are still people alive who, in 1948, were expelled from their home village of Kafr Biram in Galilee during the military operation following the establishment of the State of Israel in 1948. None of the Christian Palestinian population in Kafr Biram were subsequently permitted to return and settled in other cities and villages. Instead, a kibbutz named Bar'am was established in 1949. For the descendants, mainly

---

[6] Miroslav Volf, The End of Memory: Remembering Rightly in a Violent World. Grand Rapids, MI.: Willian B. Eerdmans, 2006, 214.

Maronites and Melkites, a common history has been established with the symbol of the church merged into their identity. Over the years, the former inhabitants have filed court cases to be allowed to return but without success. When Pope John Paul II (2000) and Pope Benedict XVI (2009) visited Israel, the villagers appealed to the Vatican for help to be able to return to Kafr Biram. At the same time, young couples have rejoiced in visiting the ruins of the village and the remaining parts of the church during celebrations. Their identity is still intricately connected to the past and to the holy site of the remains of the church and the bell-tower, which are seen as symbols of hope. The place is a holy site even for those who never inhabited in the village, as it connects the memory of the past with the present and the future.

Kafr Biram, © Göran Gunner

In other cases, survivors relocate to new locations or in a diaspora far from the original geography. The hope of those destroying holy sites seems to be that, in marginalising or wiping out parts of an area's history, the departed faith communities will forget their religious and cultural heritage. In a diasporic situation, personal identity is often closely tied to the memory of the places of worship. The past, in the form of ruins and destroyed churches, is fused into the memory of the survivors and their offspring. While a person may not live in the once inhabited area, the connection to their origin grows over the years and is passed on to subsequent generations. Photos, symbols, paintings, bibles, stories, songs are signs that can live on for generations and can also be intensified by the years. A common memory comes together like pieces of a puzzle. What happened to an individual, a family or a village blends into what happened to the people, to the entire faith community. In the meanwhile, a new narrative is built, an ideal image that is longed for. The challenge is to never forget, to commemorate the memory in various ways, and be filled with the utmost hope of once again returning to the holy site.

It seems essential to remember and, at the same time, transform the evil acts into something new. One example may be what happened in Etchmiadzin, Armenia in 2015. The Armenian Apostolic Church canonised the 1.5 million victims of the genocide.

'… [O]ne and one half million sons and daughters of our nation were subjected to slaughter, famine and disease, as they were deported and forced to march to their deaths. Centuries of honest accomplishments and creativity were swiftly plundered. Thousands of monasteries and churches were desecrated and destroyed. National institutions and schools were razed and ruined. Our spiritual and cultural treasures were uprooted and obliterated.'[7]

---

[7] Encyclical by His Holiness Karekin II Catholicos of All Armenians Dedicated to the Centennial of the Armenian Genocide. Mother See of Holy Etchmiadzin, 23 April 2015, 33.

Etchmiadzin 2015 © Göran Gunner

A painting was inaugurated during the canonisation process. On the painting are not only the individuals killed, and thus those becoming saints, but monasteries and churches no longer in existence are featured in the background. For the survivors, the holy sites function as a backdrop and can never be separated from the people; the one cannot be imagined without the other. Abuses, violations and even genocide, in combination with demolished, sacred buildings, have become an integral part of their identity.

There are legal instruments, not least in International Humanitarian Law, to protect the cultural and religious heritage of such holy sites. The regulations are treated in other parts of this publication but one non-governmental declaration is worth mentioning. *The Universal Code of Conduct on Holy Sites* was developed, in consultation with religious leaders and experts from the world's major faiths, by a working group of representatives from non-governmental organisations.[8]

---

[8] One World in Dialogue, Oslo Center for Peace and Human Rights, Religions for Peace and Search for Common Ground. Funding for the Code was received from the Norwegian Ministry of Foreign Affairs.

In the preamble of *The Universal Code of Conduct on Holy Sites*, it states that 'Holy Sites are places of profound significance and sacred religious attachment whose special character and integrity are to be preserved and protected against all violence and desecration'.[9] Holy sites have cultural value but it is human beings - individually or in community with other - that develops and maintain a religious attachment to the sites. It is significant to the establishing of the religious affiliation, the worldview and the entire identity, pinpointing the obvious importance of holy sites for individuals belonging to a faith community. The Code of Conduct shares a vision where 'the attachment of persons and communities to their holy sites is respected by everyone, regardless of their belief'. And article 2 includes:

> 'Holy sites shall be preserved for present and future generations, with dignity, integrity and respect for their name and identity. They shall be preserved both as sites of religious significance, and as historical, cultural, and ecological legacies of their communities and of humankind. They shall not be desecrated or damaged, nor shall religious communities be forcibly deprived of their holy sites.'

The destruction of holy sites can never merely be seen as an act to be forgotten in the next moment. Part of the identities of individuals and communities connected to a destroyed holy site are also destroyed. They must live with these memories, struggle with the reasons why and try to restore a life without those historical and emotional connections, and this will go on to affect and change the identity of future generations. The destruction may prevent the continuation of life in the homeland and force people into a diaspora. Article 6 in the Code of Conduct talks

---

[9] Universal Code of Conduct on Holy Sites can be downloaded at https://www.sfcg.org/wp-content/uploads/2014/06/ucchs.pdf (accessed 5 June 2016).

about both reconstruction and memorialisation: 'The relevant authorities shall take measures to facilitate the reconstruction or memorialisation of a holy site destroyed or damaged by physical violence, according to the wishes of the religious community concerned.'[10]

In conclusion, even the concept of identity is not easy to define, nor is it easy for a human being to see all the components that creates a person. Dealing with atrocities of the past, a Russian researcher declares, 'People without history are just population. But those who can tell their story – they are a people.'[11] Inheriting a wound through generations from the destruction of holy sites is a challenge, as well as an impetus to the preservation of today's holy sites for generations to come.

---

[10] Universal Code of Conduct on Holy Sites.

[11] Quoted from an article in Swedish: Laurén, Anna-Lena, 'En rättegång ska begrava sanningen om Stalins offer', in Dagens Nyheter, 18 September 2017, 16.

4

LEGAL REFLECTION: HOW CAN THE LAW UNDERSTAND AND PROTECT WHAT IS HOLY TO BELIEVERS?

Rev. Dr Patrick Roger Schnabel,
commissioned by the Protestant Church in Germany (EKD)

There is no legal definition of either 'place of worship' or 'holy site'. There is usually only one reason for the lack of a specific legal definition of a subject, which is that it is generally assumed and plausible and that the meaning is self-explanatory and unambiguous to all.

This, however, is rarely the case, and in times of increasing plurality and the subsequent erosion of self-explanatory, unambiguous concepts, it is an increasingly courageous assumption. For example, Article 6 of the German constitution provides special protection to marriage. When Parliament legislated for the opening of marriage to couples of the same sex, whether this change needed a new definition of what a marriage is on constitutional level or whether it would suffice to give a new, inclusive definition on the level of organic law was highly disputed among even the highest ranking of constitutional lawyers. Finally, it was decided to do the latter only (by adding the possibility of same-sex marriages to § 1353 Civil Code), with the reasoning that people would, within a few years, not even consider that Art. 6 might not include same-sex marriages. The reception of the term would simply differ. More conservative voices demanded a change of the constitution, as it was deemed impossible or at least improper to change the meaning of a word that has, for several thousands of years, and in different cultural and religious contexts, had only one meaning – the covenant between a man and a woman.

This example shows that it is not necessarily wise to operate with an assumption of a clear legal definition following from a common understanding of a certain linguistic term. Legal definitions do still offer room for interpretation but they are certainly more precise than those with a common understanding.

While the subjects are quite different, the issue with 'places of worship' and, quite certainly with the even less concrete concept of 'holy sites', is the same. So, how can the law deal with it?

This question is of particular importance when it comes to special protection of such places and sites. The law needs to know what it is protecting. Legal knowledge is best understood by a legal definition. Where it is lacking, the subject needs to be approached via a more indirect path. In the case of composite terms, one way is to look at the individual components and see if there are clearer definitions for those.

Starting with 'place' and 'site', even a critical interpreter would probably assume that a legal definition beyond a common understanding would probably be slightly overambitious. However, not even this might be clear in the long run: with the speedy digitalisation of our lives, and the desire of religions to keep up with this development, virtual places of worship might not be far-fetched. Certainly, activities in the digital sphere fall under the protection of law for Freedom and Belief. Now, would such a platform be considered an *activity* or a *means of communication* or a virtual *place of worship*? Will a younger generation attach any emotional affection or spiritual meaning to a virtual meeting room? No doubt someone better informed and well versed in internet law will write an intelligent article about it in due time.

The next paragraphs take a closer look at non-virtual locations.

The term place of worship should then be viewed from its second component. *Worship* is the word given to formalised rites or rituals attached to religion or belief. For a location to qualify as a place of worship, rites of this type need to be performed by different people in that place, but not necessarily by people acting together, as in typical Christian services. Shrines of other religions are often predominantly used for individual prayer and offerings but not every place where individual piety is expressed can claim special legal protection. A place does not necessarily have to be open to all nor even too many adherents of a religion or belief; in some religions, is a progressive initiation process needed in order to gain access to the sanctuary or inner sanctum, with access limited to a small minority. Nevertheless, such altars would be regarded as places of worship and hold meaning to more people than solely those who worship there.

The next question, and here the legal reasoning is quite close to the theological reasoning touched on previously, is when and how does a place of worship become a place of worship? Many would agree that worship can be performed almost anywhere but not every place would then become a place of worship. This idea could be better understood via the old joke of the Benedictine and the Jesuit, both of whom enjoy smoking. They argue whether smoking and praying at the same time is allowed. In the end, they each decide to write to the Holy Father in Rome. When they meet again the Benedictine says, 'See, I was right. Smoking whilst praying is not allowed!'. The Jesuit says, 'No, no, I was right. It is allowed!'. When they compare letters, they find that the Benedictine has asked for permission to smoke while praying, while the Jesuit has asked for permission to pray while smoking.

Likewise, worship is possible in any place but this does not transform any place into a place of worship, thus demonstrating that even the seemingly simple term of place of worship can be difficult to define legally. This is even truer of holy site.

While *site* is quite clearly referring to a specific location, *holy* is far more diluted and evasive than *worship*. In different religions and, indeed, even in Christian history, there are holy mountains, holy lands, even holy rivers. This renders its general legal protection almost impossible.

When focusing on the familiar concept of Holy Land, does the theological concept of holiness oblige a state or international community to offer legal protection to adherents of a religion that so claims a land? What if several religions were to claim the same land as their holy land? This constellation is tragically realistic and a source of great contention between the (religious) descendants of Abraham.

Likewise, what would a protection of the Ganges, the holy river of the Hindu religion, look like? Would a right of access at certain places suffice or would it have to include even better environmental protection so people may safely bathe?

This is in no way an attempt to ridicule any existing concept of holiness. The intention is simply to draw attention to how difficult it is to compress 'holy site' into a legal definition and, even more difficult, to describe in what way effective legal protection and remedy could be implemented.

Therefore, with respect to the wider understanding of place of worship or holy site and the attached difficulties, this article will now solely focus further deductions and analysis strictly to buildings and artificially built monuments that serve or have continuously served as places of worship for a religious or belief-based community.

How can such buildings or monuments become a place of worship or holy site that deserves special legal protection?

In the context of Christian churches, the need for some sort of formal consecration or dedication is usually assumed. Canon or ecclesiastical laws have been very influential in the development of secular law. It would be easy to conclude that any structure especially consecrated or dedicated to worship by the competent authorities, and duly registered in the ecclesiastical records, should be regarded as a place of worship or holy site and given special protection. This is how it has worked traditionally; a classic example is the English 'Places of Worship Registration Act', last revised in 1855.

However, in a religiously pluralistic society, this notion could seem somewhat church-centric. With this in mind, reverting to another determining factor is recommendable, that of reverting to the legal figure of *religious self-understanding.*

In the German legal tradition, the concept of the state as secular implies that it cannot assume defamatory powers in areas of religion or belief. Religion and belief are inherent characteristics of person and society, prior to any state and its law. The state is required to protect what it finds, not to define what it wants to protect. It is those who bear the fundamental right to Freedom of Religion or Belief who define what their religion is and entails.

There are, of course, limits with respect to this concept of religious self-understanding. While the state must not judge religious content, it must surely be able to prevent abuse. The law must know what it is to protect. Religious freedom is not carte blanche to do anything on a whim, claiming it is religion based. Again, there is no clear-cut legal definition of religion or belief but the law uses concepts of other professions such a theology, religious studies, sociology, psychology etc. to arrive at a well-founded understanding of what phenomena must be protected as religious and which are fraudulent. Within the limits of what the state can reasonably be asked and expected to protect in terms of religion, religious communities and associations have the right to define the contents of their beliefs, including the question of how a special religious significance becomes attached to a building or monument that needs to be respected as such.

However, the law cannot evade further considerations. It is certainly neither necessary nor, on the other hand, an improper infringement of Freedom of Religion or Belief, to ask religious communities to have places of worship or holy sites registered as such, as per the aforementioned English 'Places of Worship Registration Act 1855'. That does not necessarily mean that only such duly registered sites generally qualify as places of worship; the state may make registration obligatory for certain rights attached to such a qualification. It is doubtful, though, that legal protection can be totally denied to all such places that are not duly registered under such a legal regime.

That certainly holds true where no equivalent registration requirement is imposed. In this case, the state will have to look for other objective criteria along with 'self-understanding' of the religious community.

Two examples will follow. The first is related to property rights, the second to usage. Property rights here refer to the religious communities' legitimate claim to such a building or monument. When the community is not its actual owner, it must at least have a right to its use. Good examples are churches in France built prior to 1901, which have officially been appropriated by the state but have been left to liturgical use by the church they belonged to before secularisation. If such rights are unattested and therefore contested, special attention must be given to tradition and must, at the least, never be discriminatory, and the legal dispossession of property used for religious purposes becomes far more difficult than with any other property.

The second criterion is usage. A church or religious community might own several buildings whereof some have not been dedicated to religious purposes. In order to qualify, the respective building would need to have a proven track record of religious usage. Again, this is easier to prove for religious communities that have a concept of consecration or dedication, but some sort of proof is a prerequisite for any religious community.

This is not an exhaustive analysis on legal definitions of places of worship or holy sites. There are lines of thought that have been omitted which did not seem pertinent to the core legal issue at hand.

One does deserve to be mentioned, at least in passing, which is that of cultural heritage. It is not a criterion relating to religion in the stricter sense of the meaning, i.e. in the legal sense, but it is relevant to this discussion. For most historic religions, several holy sites have an added value in cultural heritage. They can be listed buildings or listed under UNESCO world cultural heritage sites. As far as legal protection is concerned, this certainly gives weight to the level of protection. In a ground-breaking judgement, the International Criminal Court has only recently declared the destruction of religious sites belonging to the cultural heritage of a people and region as a crime against humanity.

When looking at many countries' penal codes, even expressly secularist countries such as France,[1] a special protection is provided to places of worship. To obstruct religious ceremony, steal from a church, desecrate a shrine, destroy a temple, is considered a more severe crime than the obstruction of a secular meeting, theft, damage to property or the destruction of a building.[2]

In times of pluralism, of increasing migration, and in times where religion is being increasingly drawn into cultural conflict, it would be wise to come to clearer definitions of places of worship and holy sites in national and in international law. This, and only this, can properly prepare the ground for protection that is urgently needed.

At the beginning of this millennium, the Lord's Select Committee on Religious Offences in England and Wales concluded, 'Whether places

---

[1] cf. Code pénal 2016, Art. 461-13

[2] cf. StGB Deutschland, §§ 167, 243, 306a; StGB Österreich §§ 126, 128, 189; artt. 195/196 Criminal Code of Poland; 18 U.S. Code § 247

of worship, of all faiths, need a modern protection in criminal law is something which has become increasingly marginal'[3].

That was quite certainly a serious misjudgement of the situation.

The UN Human Rights Committee seems more realistic, which, in its resolution 6/37, urged States 'to exert the utmost efforts, in accordance with their national legislation and in conformity with international human rights and humanitarian law, to ensure that religious places, sites, shrines and symbols are fully respected and protected and to take additional measures in cases where they are vulnerable to desecration or destruction', reaffirming the 1981 General Assembly declaration that the fundamental right to Freedom of Religion or Belief includes the right 'to establish and maintain places for these purposes' and that 'the concept of worship extends to the building of places of worship'. With regard to situations of conflict, it is also important to take notice of the 2017 UN Security Council resolution 2347, which: 'deplores and condemns the unlawful destruction of cultural heritage, inter alia destruction of religious sites and artefacts', emphasising 'that the unlawful destruction of cultural heritage, and the looting and smuggling of cultural property in the event of armed conflicts, notably by terrorist groups, and the attempt to deny historical roots and cultural diversity in this context can fuel and exacerbate conflict and hamper post-conflict national reconciliation, thereby undermining the security, stability, governance, social, economic and cultural development of affected States'.

---

[3] House of Lords Session 2002–03 Select Committee on Religious Offences in England and Wales, Volume I, report (HL Paper 95–I), source https://publications.parliament.uk/pa/ld200203/ldselect/ldrelof/95/9512.htm, last opened 25/11/2020.

PART III

EXISTING FRAMEWORKS
FOR THE PROTECTION OF PLACES
OF WORSHIP AND HOLY SITES

*Different National Legislation from Europe
and the Middle East*

5

FRANCE

Willy Fautré, Human Rights without Frontiers

The issue of the protection of holy places and places of worship is usually raised in areas and countries affected by war. France is not at war with any country but, in the last few years, the country has been a main target of Islamist terrorist attacks. Individuals and groups motivated by feelings of hate against a specific religious group have also targeted religious buildings and threatened clerics and believers during religious services.

1. Protection of Religious Community Buildings

According to Ministry of Interior statistics published on 1 February 2017, 4320 places of worship and religious community buildings were under surveillance and under the protection of mobile (non-static) law enforcement patrols and military forces in 2016:

- 2400 out of 45,000 Christian sites (5%)
- 1100 out of 2500 Muslim sites (44%)
- 820 Jewish synagogues, schools and community centres (100%).

Moreover, in the last two years, a 12.5 million EUR budget was approved for the purchase of security and video-protection material for the most sensitive religious sites.

It is noteworthy that soldiers protecting religious buildings were targets of physical attacks. On 3 February 2015, three soldiers guarding a Jewish community centre in Nice were targeted in a knife attack; on 1 January 2016, a man tried to run down troops guarding a mosque in Valence.

In 2016, incidents targeting Jewish and Muslim community buildings decreased by 54% and 37.5% respectively in comparison with 2015, while there was a 17.4% increase concerning Christian (Catholic) places of worship:[1] 949 incidents according to the Ministry of Interior, including 399 acts of vandalism and 191 cases of theft of items of worship.[2]

The Ministry of Interior also notes that fourteen incidents were motivated by Satanism, with an anarchist connotation in twenty-five cases, but most of the time the perpetrators and their motivations remain unknown.

These statistical ups and downs follow the same trend as global statistics on anti-Semitic, anti-Muslim, and anti-Christian incidents.

2. Anti-Semitic, Anti-Muslim, and Anti-Christian Incidents

After a record number of reported racist, anti-Semitic and anti-Muslim incidents in 2015 (2034 incidents), their number largely de-

---

[1] En 2016, les actes racistes, antisémites et antimusulmans ont baissé en France mais pas les actes antichrétiens, France-Info, 1 février 2017, http://bit.ly/2I9GWS2

[2] A closer look at the statistics indicates that from 2008 to 2016, reported incidents concerning Christian places of worship increased by 245 %.

creased in 2016 with 1125 reported incidents (-44.7%).[3] The French government sees this drop as 'the fruit of government initiatives', in particular a 100 million EUR campaign to 'fight racism, anti-Semitism and all forms of discrimination linked to origin or religion'[4].

3. Religiously Motivated Attacks and Incidents in Churches in 2016-2017

On 26 July 2016, Father Jacques Hamel, an 86-year old Catholic priest, was stabbed to death by two young, French Muslims during a church service in Saint-Étienne-du-Rouvray and a churchgoer was wounded. Both aggressors were shot dead by police.[5]

In October 2016, a 22-year-old Moroccan was sentenced to six months in prison for attempting to burn down several churches.[6] A month prior, he was reported to have set fire to two churches in Millau, in southern France: the Sacré-Coeur church and the Notre-Dame de l'Espinasse, 400 meters away. French police then placed the third church in Millau under surveillance and arrested the man as he attempted to burn it down. The police did not communicate these acts of van-

---

[3] Baisse des actes racistes, antisémites et antimusulmans en 2016, Gouvernement français, 1 février 2017, http://bit.ly/2lxufld. Sortie du Rapport 2017 du CCIF : une évolution du fait islamophobe, http://bit.ly/2gankNa

[4] Cf. e.g. https://www.lefigaro.fr/flash-actu/2017/02/01/97001-20170201FILW WW00052-net-recul-des-actes-racistes-en-2016.php.

[5] Le Père Jacques Hamel, un homme bon mais qui ne transigeait pas, Le Monde, 7 août 2016 http://www.lemonde.fr/religions/article/2016/08/07/le-pere-jacques-hamel-un-homme-bon-mais-qui-ne-transige-pas_4979475_1653130.html. Abdel Kermiche et Abdel Malik Petitjean, tueurs de l'église de St-Etienne-du-Rouvray, L'Express, 18 août 2016.

[6] Six mois de prison pour des incendies dans des églises, Le Figaro, 12 octobre 2017, http://www.lefigaro.fr/flash-actu/2016/10/12/97001-20161012FILWWW 00341-6-mois-de-prison-pour-des-incendies-dans-des-eglises.php

dalism and the name of the perpetrator was not revealed in the French media.

On 2 April 2017, there was an arson attempt against the Armenian Evangelical Church in Alfortville (Val-de-Marne).[7] A garbage can was filled with petrol in front of the building and set on fire. Pastor Gilbert Léonian expressed his anger in the media because the local authorities had not taken action after acts of vandalism had been perpetrated against the same building on 26 February. The pastor did not rule out that the attacks might have been motivated by his having invited pastor Norek Hovsétian, of the Armenian Evangelical Church in Baghdad, to a series of conferences in France on the situation of Christians in the Middle East.

On 23 April 2017, a young Muslim woman entered the Catholic church of Rennes-le-Château with an axe, attacked the stoup, decapitated the famous red devil of the Bible Asmodea attached to it, cut off his arm, put a Koran on it, and lacerated the bas-relief of the altar.[8] Worshippers immediately called the mayor and she was arrested. When asked why she had committed such a crime, she calmly answered, 'Today is election day here but in Syria the West is bombing and killing children. You are all *kafirs*! My husband is over there'. She was examined by psychiatrists and declared accountable for her acts. After her arrest, she was placed in police custody and then referred to the Office of the Public Prosecutor in Carcassonne. At her trial on 27 October, the woman, who was a law firm employee, recused her lawyer, Hichem Laredj, and defended herself. She admitted that her act had been premeditated and was symbolic. The court sentenced the woman, known only as

---

[7] Alfortville: Incendie criminel à l'église évangélique arménienne, Le Parisien, 2 avril 2017 http://www.leparisien.fr/alfortville-94140/alfortville-incendie-criminel-a-l-eglise-evangelique-armenienne-02-04-2017-6818292.php

[8] Diable décapité, le procès ce matin, La Dépêche, 8 septembre 2017 http://www.ladepeche.fr/article/2017/09/08/2640955-diable-decapite-le-proces-ce-matin.html#xtor=EPR-1

Kenza, to a suspended two-year prison term and an amount of 17,718 EUR to repair the damaged statue. She was also prohibited from appearing in Rennes-le-Château. The judgment was publicised on 27 November.

4. Other Religions

No other religious group, with the exception of Jehovah's Witnesses, has collected and publicised any data relating to incidents aiming at the damage or destruction of places of worship or other religious community buildings. Between January 2016 and July 2017, they recorded about fifteen cases of vandalism and arson attempts. They filed criminal complaints but claim that law enforcement officials have failed to investigate the incidents properly and prosecute the perpetrators.

5. No Impunity

Acts of violence targeting places of worship and religious meetings cannot remain unpunished and must be tackled with determination by law enforcement and the judiciary, whatever the religious or belief group.

France's criminal code does not have any specific provisions against vandalism and (attempted) acts of total or partial destruction of places of worship and religious community buildings but such incidents can be prosecuted on the basis of general articles:

Article 322-1 (and 4): Vandalism (attempts)
- Minimum: A fine of 3750 EUR and community service
- Maximum: A two-year prison term and a fine of 30,000 EUR

Article 322-6 (and 11): Destruction and arson (attempts)
- Maximum: A 10-year prison term and a fine of 150,000 EUR

France prosecutes perpetrators of acts of vandalism against religious buildings when identified and abides by the strong recommendations of UN Special Rapporteur on Freedom of Religion or Belief, Heiner Bielefeldt (2010-2016), who stated in his report on the prevention of violence committed in the name of religion (Document 1: A/HRC/28/66)[9]. Para 90:

> 'States have the obligation to act swiftly to stop acts of violence committed in the name of religion, against individuals, groups and places of worship. Overcoming a culture of impunity, wherever it exists, must be a priority. Those who commit or are complicit in acts of violence must be brought to justice.'

However, it must be noted that the national media and news outlets usually keep silent on acts of vandalism and desecration in Catholic churches while they are swift to denounce anti-Jewish and anti-Muslim incidents.

---

[9] http://www.ohchr.org/Documents/Issues/Religion/A-HRC-28-66_en.doc

6

RUSSIA

The Concept and Nature of Real Estate Objects for Religious Purposes According to the Legislation of the Russian Federation.

Prof. Dr Igor V. Ponkin, IPACS of the RANEPA,
His Eminence, Dr Metropolitan of Smolensk and Dorogobuzh
Isidor (Tupikin Roman), Diocesan Bishop of the Smolensk Dio-
cese and Fr. Dr Vladislav Bagan, Secretary of the Smolensk
Diocesan Administration

According to paragraph 1 of Article 2 of the Federal Act of the Russian Federation, dated 30 November, 2010, No. 327-FZ (as amended on 23 June, 2014) on Restitution of Religious Property in State or Municipal Ownership to Religious Organisations,

'real estate objects for religious purposes are: facilities, buildings, structures, constructions, including Russian Federation cultural heritage sites (historical and cultural sites), monasteries, temples, and/or other religious complexes, built to practice and/or support activities of religious organisations such as worship, other religious rites and ceremonies, prayer and religious meetings, religious education, professional religious training, monastic life, pilgrimage - including buildings for temporary accommodation of pilgrims, as well as movable religious property (objects of interior decoration of religious buildings and structures, objects intended for worship and other religious purposes)'.

In 1903, I.S. Berdnikov wrote that

'Among human needs, satisfaction of which is ensured by law, [an important place] belongs to religious needs. Consistent with their nature, people satisfy their religious need not only spiritually, in their minds and hearts, but also externally by worshipping God and following His commandments. Furthermore, people cannot do without communication with others of their kind in divine worship, as well as in satisfying their other needs. Thus, several legal relations arise from satisfying people's religious needs, as happens when satisfying their other needs. Together they constitute an especially complex legal institution'.[1]

The issue regarding the position and value of property relations within the total scope of the relations of religious organisations with the state, with other persons, in terms of the content of such relations, is one of the most difficult in civil law science, as well as in the field of realisation of freedom of religion and state-confessional relations. The property of a religious organisation consists of property (religious or otherwise) owned on the grounds of property rights. In the case of a complex religious organisation (centralised religious organisation like a diocese), its property are those belonging to all legal entities operating within the framework of the organisation or, with a wider approach, to all entities associated with it (that is, property that a religious organisation controls indirectly). The legal nature of religious property and, most importantly, the imperatives of recognizing its specifics by the state are largely de-

---

[1] Berdnikov I.S. Brief Course of Church Law of the Orthodox Church. 2nd edition, revised and enlarged – Kazan: Typo-lithography of the Imperial University, 1903 – 333pp., p. 1.

termined by the autonomy of the internal orders established within religious organisations.

An autonomous extra-legal normative order in the field of religion is formed in an elaborately ontological way. It is determined, *inter alia*, by a complex of guarantees of the autonomy of religious associations. This complex determines the checks (limits of interference) of state authorities in their intervention in internal affairs and the rule-making competence of religious associations (these guarantees result in the guarantees of state non-interference in these matters) and also has a definitive impact on the legal status of religious property.

Among the guarantees of autonomy for religious associations in the legislation of the Russian Federation there are:

- Legal guarantees of the collective freedom of religion (Article 28 of the Constitution of the Russian Federation, a number of articles of the Federal Act 'On the Freedom of Conscience and Religious Associations';

- Legal guarantees of separation of religious associations from the state, determined by the Secularity of the State (Articles 14 and 28 of the Constitution of the Russian Federation, paragraphs 1 and 2 of Article 4 of the Federal Act 'On the Freedom of Conscience and Religious Associations'), which define the autonomy of their activities and a certain scope of self-regulatory powers; this guarantee is strengthened by the8 prohibition of other laws to contradict the guarantees of the Federal Act 'On the Freedom of Conscience and Religious Associations', established by paragraph 2 of Article 2 of the Federal Act 'On the Freedom of Conscience and Religious Associations';[2]

---

[2] See: Ponkin I.V. Secularity: Constitutional-Legal Study / Institute of relations between the State and religious denominations and Law. – Moscow: Associations, 2002. – 308 p. Ponkin I.V. Legal Grounds of secularity of the State and Education. – Moscow: Pro-Press, 2003. – 416 p. Ponkin I.V. Secularity of the

- Legal guarantees on the freedom for everyone not to be forced to report their attitude to religion, to determine their attitude to religion, to practice or refuse to practice religion, to participate in worship or not, other religious rites and ceremonies, in the activities of religious associations, to religion education (paragraph 5 of Article 3 of the Federal Act 'On the Freedom of Conscience and Religious Associations');

- Legal guarantees of the establishment of religious associations and their activities in accordance with their own hierarchical and institutional structures (subparagraph 1 of paragraph 5 of Article 4 of the Federal Act 'On the Freedom of Conscience and Religious Associations');

- Legal guarantees for religious associations to choose, appoint, and replace their personnel in accordance with the relevant conditions and requirements and in the manner provided for by their internal regulations (unnumbered first subparagraph of paragraph 5 of Article 4 of the Federal Act 'On the Freedom of Conscience and Religious Associations');[3]

- A guarantee of respect by the state for internal normative regulations (self-regulation norms, *Lex Canonica*) of religious organisations, if these regulations do not contradict the legislation of the

State / Institute of relations between the State and religious denominations and Law. – Moscow: Publishing House of the Educational Scientific Centre of Pre-University Education, 2004. – 466 p. Ponkin I.V. Modern Secular State: Reasonable secularity. Constitutional-Legal Study – Moscow: Institute of relations between the State and religious denominations and Law, 2006. – 390 p. Ponkine I.V. Bref aperçu de la législation sur la laïcité de l'Etat en Russie. – Moscou: Centre de science et de l'enseignement pré-supérieure, 2005, p.96

[3] See: Ponkin I.V., Ryabykh Pp., Ponkina A.I. Sur la reconnaissance de la compétence exclusive des groupements religieux afin d'instaurer leur structure intrinsèque et les normes intérieures des relations en tant qu'une des garanties de la liberté de la conscience dans l'État démocratique // Stato, Chiese e pluralismo confessionale. – 12 novembre 2012. – No. 34.

Russian Federation (paragraph 2 of Article 15 of the Federal Act 'On the Freedom of Conscience and Religious Associations');

- A guarantee of free operation of religious organisations in accordance with their internal regulations, if they do not contradict the legislation of the Russian Federation, and have the legal capacity provided for in their charters (paragraph 2 of Article 15 of the Federal Act 'On the Freedom of Conscience and Religious Associations');

- A guarantee for religious organisations to freely establish, in accordance with their internal regulations, the conditions for the activities of clergy and religious personnel, as well as the requirements for them, including the issues of religious education (paragraph 5 of Article 24 of the Federal Act 'On the Freedom of Conscience and Religious Associations').

The nature of the specifics of real estate objects for religious purposes (buildings, constructions, land plots) is determined by the value of these objects, which is unique in the legal framework. They are centres of attraction, convergence within the collective actualisation of the freedom of religion, unique material and property sites (universes), which are attributed by the believers with special (according to the perception of believers, i.e. spiritual) properties that make these sites (inside and/or in the immediate vicinity of the site, on the surface of the land plot or above it) the objects of particular sensitivity for religious feelings of believers and, therefore, the objects of special (having a fiduciary nature) state obligations for increased legal protection and support. Accordingly, state recognition of the norms of religious organisations concerning the normative position and the value of real estate objects for religious purposes and implementation of the relevant imperatives for itself (meaning special, mainly fiduciary, attitude of the state to such property) is determined by the following:

- Recognition and presumption of the value of real estate objects for religious purposes in the perception of believers as arising from their acceptance of voluntary obligations (when expressing membership in a religious organisation) and acceptance (as mandatory) of the order and internal regulations of a religious organisation, positioning and presuming a special religiously revered (subject to religious veneration) nature of such property. For believers, it is impossible to belittle the value and perception of an item of religious property, as, among other things, this would be a gross violation of the internal regulatory framework of their religious organisation. In this case, the corresponding value for the state is regressively predetermined by the imperatives of a certain recognition and respect by the state for the internal regulations and the internal order of a religious organisation;
- Recognition and presumption of the actual value of real estate objects for religious purposes for religious feelings of believers; the corresponding value for the state in this case is regressively determined by imperatives of respect by the state for religious feelings and the personal dignity of believers, legal protection and support thereof;
- Recognition and presumption of the significance of the norms of religious organisations (*Lex Canonica*) regarding real estate objects for religious purposes as 'order-forming' and 'order-keeping' values in the conditions of the reduced capabilities of the secular state to substantially (and, even more, fully) administer this field of relations, including the instruments of civil law nature.[4]

---

[4] Isidor, Metropolitan of Smolensk and Dorogobuzh (Tupikin R.V.) Real estate objects for religious purposes: Foreign Regulation Experience / Edited by M.N. Kuznetsov / Institute of relations between the State and religious denominations and Law. – Smolensk: Svitok, 2019. – 320 p. – P. 52–53.

Structure and Description of Normative Legal Regulation of the Legal Status of Real Estate Objects for Religious Purposes in Russia

It follows from Article 71 and part 3 of Article 55 of the Constitution of the Russian Federation, which regulation in this area is assigned mainly to the federal level of state power. This does not exclude certain legal opportunities for the constituent entities of the Russian Federation in cooperation with federal authorities, arising from article 72 of the Constitution of the Russian Federation, which was fully expressed in the field of returning religious property by the state or municipalities to religious organisations.

The legal status of religious property in Russia is determined by the reference articles relevant to the topic of study of the Constitution of the Russian Federation (Articles 28 and 14) and, indirectly, by a number of other constitutional articles (Articles 17, 18, 55, etc.), as well as the following normative legal acts:

The basic Act in this area:

- Federal Act (Federal Law), 26 September 1997, No. 125-FZ (amended 02 December 2019) 'On the Freedom of Conscience and Religious Associations' (the norms of Federal Act, 12 January 1996, N 7-FZ, amended 12 December 2019, 'On Non-Profit Organisations' are also applied)

Regarding the basic civil law status of religious sites (estate objects for religious purposes):

- Part One of the Civil Code of the Russian Federation, 30 November 1994, No. 51-FZ, as amended on 16 December 2019; Article 22 (amended 3 August 2018) of the Federal Act, 30 November 1994, No. 52-FZ 'On the enactment of Part One of the Civil Code of the Russian Federation' removed 'buildings erected without proper legal authorisation as part of religious property in accordance with the Federal Act, as well as intended for servicing religious property and/or forming one monastery, temple or other complex of religious worship' from the scope of paragraph 4 of Article 222 of the Civil Code of the Russian Federation, which determines the legal status of unauthorised buildings and the conditions for their demolition;

Regarding land-legal relations and legal relations related to forest resources:

- The Land Code of the Russian Federation, 25 October 2001, No. 136-FZ (amended 18 March 2020), *inter alia*, directly - subparagraph 4 of paragraph 1 of Article 1, paragraphs 2 and 8 of Article 39.5, subparagraph 17 of paragraph 2 of Article 39.6, subparagraphs 3 and 4 of paragraph 2 of Article 39.10, paragraph 1 of Article 78;
- Forest Code of the Russian Federation, 4 December 2006, No. 200-FZ (amended 27 December 2018), *inter alia*, directly - paragraph 7 of part 1 of Article 21, paragraph 15 of part 1 of Article 25, Article 47 'Use of Forests for Religious Activities';

Regarding the return of religious property by the state to religious organisations:

- Federal Act of the Russian Federation, 30 November 2010, No. 327-FZ (amended 23 June 2014) 'On Restitution of Religious Property in State or Municipal Ownership to Religious Organisations';
- Order of the Government of the Russian Federation, 30 December 2011, No. 1226 'On Approval of the Rules for the Formation and Publication of the Plan of the Restitution of Religious Property in State or Municipal Ownership to Religious Organisations';

- Order of the Government of the Russian Federation, 30 June 2001, No. 490 (amended 21 April 2011) 'On the Procedure of the Restitution of Religious Property in State or Municipal Ownership to Religious Organisations under Federal Ownership, Assigned to Museum Objects and Museum Collections Included in the State Part of the Museum Fund of the Russian Federation or the Documents of the Archive Fund of the Russian Federation';

- Order of the Government of the Russian Federation, 26 April 2011, No. 325 (amended 10 May 2016) 'On the List of Documents Justifying the Right of a Religious Organisation to Receive Public or Municipal Religious Property and the Procedure for their Release';

- Order of the Government of the Russian Federation, 26 April 2011, No. 324 'On Federal Executive Bodies Authorised to Exercise Certain Powers in Order to Implement the Federal Act' on 'Restitution of Religious Property in State or Municipal Ownership to Religious Organisations';

- Order of the Government of the Russian Federation, 12 August 2011, No. 678 'On Approval of the Regulation on the Commission on Issues Arising during the Review of Applications of Religious Organisations for the Restitution of Religious Property under Federal Ownership';

- Order of the Ministry of Economic Development of the Russian Federation, 3 March 2014, No. 102 'On Approval of the Administrative Regulation Regarding the Provision by the Federal Agency for State Property Management of the State Service for the Provision of Religious Organisations with Ownership or Free Use of Federal Religious Property', as well as Federal property that meets the criteria established by part 3 of Article 5 and/or part 1 of Article 12 of Federal Act, 30 November 2010, No. 327-

FZ 'On Restitution of Religious Property in State or Municipal Ownership to Religious Organisations'.

Regarding fire safety issues:

- Federal Act, 22 July 2008, No. 123-FZ (amended 27 December 2018) 'Technical Regulations on Fire Safety Requirements' (part 5 of Article 1, subparagraph 'ж' of paragraph 3 of part 1 of Article 32);

- Order of the Government of the Russian Federation, 25 April 2012, No. 390 (amended 20 September 2019) 'On the Fire Safety Regime' (together with the 'Rules of the Fire Prevention Regime in the Russian Federation' - Section XXI 'Real Estate for Religious Purposes';

- Orders of the Ministry of the Russian Federation for Civil Defence, Emergencies and Elimination of Consequences of Natural Disasters (the MES of Russia), 23 November 2016, No. 615 'On Approval of the Rules Real Estate for Religious Purposes. Fire Safety Requirements' and No. 332, 13 August 2018 'On Approval of the Rules Cultural Heritage Real Estate for Religious Purposes. Fire Safety Requirements' (together with 'СП 388.1311500.2018. Rules. Religious Cultural Heritage Sites. Fire Safety Requirements').

Regarding binding of Real Estate for Religious Purposes by a special regime of legal protection as objects of cultural heritage:

- Federal Act, 25 June 2002, No. 73-FZ (amended 18 July 2019) 'On Cultural Heritage Sites (historical and cultural sites) of the Peoples of the Russian Federation', a number of other acts.

Regarding the tax regime:

- The Tax Code of the Russian Federation (Part Two), 5 August 2000, No. 117-FZ (amended 1 April 2020) (subparagraphs 15 of paragraph 2 and subparagraphs 1 of paragraph 3 of Article 149, subparagraph 1 of paragraph 1 of Article 219 and other).

Regarding ensuring anti-terrorism security:

- Order of the Government of the Russian Federation, 5 September 2019, No. 1165 'On Approval of the Requirements for Anti-Terrorism Protection of Sites (Territories) of Religious Organisations and the Form of a Safety Certificate of Sites (Territories) of Religious Organisations', a number of other acts.

There are several acts that are applied to religious facilities in terms of electricity, sewage, water, etc..

With all these acts, the civil law regime of real estate objects for religious purposes of the Russian Orthodox Church, as well as other major religious organisations in the Russian Federation, is characterised by a significant degree of uncertainty and gaps. Real estate objects for religious purposes, especially those owned by the state or municipalities and considered the objects of cultural heritage (historical and cultural sites), may be simultaneously covered, and often are, with intersectional (convergent, overlapping) and combinatorial (complex combined) regulation of several different legal regimes. Moreover, the clarification of the legal status of such objects is often quite accidental and depends on the specific situation. The interrelation of the norms of various legal regimes is not properly regulated and is often vague, contradictory, and conflicting.

The Legal Regime Established by the Federal Act 'On the Freedom of Conscience and Religious Associations' for Real Estate Objects for Religious Purposes

According to paragraph 1 of Article 16 of the Federal Act 'On the Freedom of Conscience and Religious Associations', religious organisations have the right to establish and maintain religious buildings and structures, other sites and objects specially used for worship, prayer, and religious meetings and religious veneration (pilgrimage).

According to paragraph 2 of Article 16 of the Federal Act, religious worship and other religious rites and ceremonies shall be unhindered in:

- Worship premises, buildings, and structures, as well as on land plots where such buildings and structures are located.
- In buildings and structures owned by religious organisations on the basis of ownership rights, or provided to them under other property rights, for the implementation of their statutory activities, as well as on land plots on which such buildings and structures are located.
- In premises owned by religious organisations on the basis of ownership rights or provided to them under other property rights to carry out their statutory activities, as well as on land plots on which buildings with the respective premises are located, upon agreement with the owners of such buildings.
- In premises, buildings, structures, and on land plots owned under the ownership right or provided under other property rights to organisations created by religious organisations;
- On land plots owned under the ownership right or provided to them under other property rights.
- In places of pilgrimage.
- In cemeteries and crematoriums.
- In residential premises.

In accordance with paragraphs 3 and 4 of Article 16 of the Federal Act, religious organisations have the right to hold religious rites and ceremonies in treatment and prophylactic and medical institutions, orphanages, nursing homes for the elderly and disabled, at the request of citizens residing in them and in rooms specially allocated for these purposes by their administration. In penitentiary institutions, religious rites, ceremonies, and personal meetings are carried out in compliance with the requirements of the penal legislation of the Russian Federation. Conducting religious rites and ceremonies on the premises of places of detention is allowed; it is carried out in accordance with the requirements of the criminal procedure legislation of the Russian Federation. Religious rites and ceremonies may also be held in buildings, religious structures located on the territories of educational organisations, as well as in the premises of educational organisations historically used for religious ceremonies. The command of military units, with adherence to the requirements of military regulations, does not impede the participation of military personnel in worship services or other religious rites and ceremonies.

Paragraph 5 of Article 16 of the Federal Act 'On the Freedom of Conscience and Religious Associations' establishes that, 'In other cases, public worship, other religious rites and ceremonies (including prayer and religious meetings), held in public places in conditions that require the measures to be adopted, which are aimed at ensuring public order and security of participants of religious rites and ceremonies, as well as of others citizens, shall be carried out in the manner prescribed for rallies, marches, and demonstrations.'

Articles 17.1 and 18 of the Federal Act determine the legal regulation, respectively, of pilgrimage and charitable and cultural-educational activities of religious organisations. Article 19 of the Federal Act determines the legal status of religious educational organisations for the training of ministers and religious personnel of religious organisations. In some cases, these articles are relevant to the issues discussed in this material.

Article 21 'Ownership Rights of Religious Organisations' of the Federal Act 'On the Freedom of Conscience and Religious Associations' establishes that religious organisations have the right to own buildings, land plots, objects of industrial, social, charitable, cultural, educational, and other functions, religious objects, monetary funds, and other property necessary to support their activities, including objects related to historical and cultural sites. Religious organisations have the ownership right to property acquired or created by them at their own expense, donated by citizens, organisations or transferred to religious organisations by the state to be owned by them, or acquired in other ways that are not contrary to the legislation of the Russian Federation. The transfer, in the established manner, to religious organisations of religious state of municipal buildings and structures with related land plots and other religious property is free of charge. Religious organisations may own property abroad. Movable property and real estate objects for worship purposes cannot be levied on claims of creditors. The list of types of property for worship purposes, which cannot be levied on claims of creditors, is established by the government of the Russian Federation following the suggestions of religious organisations.

According to Article 21.1 'Disposal of Property Owned by Religious Organisations' of the Federal Act 'On the Freedom of Conscience and Religious Associations', transactions for the disposal of real estate objects, including transactions aimed at its alienation, acquisition, lease, gratuitous use, as well as loan agreements and credit contracts, shall also be concluded by a religious organisation with the written approval of the authority of the religious organisation, authorised by the Charter of the religious organisation to issue the written approval for such transactions (the authorised body of a religious organisation). A transaction made without the approval of the authorised body of a religious organisation is void. Claims to consider such a transaction as invalid and/or to apply the consequences of its invalidity may be submitted by the party to the transaction and/or a centralised religious organisation, which includes a religious organisation that is a party to the transaction. Real estate objects for worship purposes, including objects of cultural heritage (historical and cultural sites) of the peoples of the Russian Federation, owned

by a religious organisation, in cases provided for by the Charter of a religious organisation, may be alienated by a religious organisation solely
into state or municipal ownership or into the ownership of a religious
organisation of the corresponding confession.

Article 22:

> 'Disposal of Property Owned by State, Citizens, and their Asso-
> ciations' of the Federal Act 'On the Freedom of Conscience and
> Religious Associations' establishes that, 'Religious organisations
> have the right to use for their needs land plots, buildings and
> property provided to them by state, municipal, public and other
> organisations, and citizens in accordance with the legislation of
> the Russian Federation. The transfer, in accordance with the es-
> tablished procedure, of religious buildings and structures with re-
> lated land plots, and other religious property owned by the state
> or municipal authorities to be used by religious organisations is
> free of charge.'

According to paragraph 2 of Article 24.1 of the Federal Act 'On the
Freedom of Conscience and Religious Associations', the missionary activity of a religious association shall be carried out freely in:

- Religious premises, buildings, and structures, as well as on land
  plots where such buildings and structures are located.
- Buildings and structures owned by religious organisations on the
  basis of ownership rights or provided to them under other property rights for the implementation of their statutory activities, as
  well as on land plots on which such buildings and structures are
  located.
- Premises owned by religious organisations on the basis of ownership rights or provided to them under other property rights to carry out their statutory activities, as well as on land plots on which

buildings with the respective premises are located, upon agreement with the owners of such buildings.

- Premises, buildings, structures and land plots owned under the ownership right or provided under other property rights to organisations created by religious organisations; on land plots owned by them under the ownership right or provided to them under other property rights;
  - o Places of pilgrimage.
  - o Cemeteries and crematoriums.
  - o Premises of educational organisations.
  - o Premises historically used for religious ceremonies.

Moreover, paragraph 1 of Article 24.1 defines missionary activity as follows: 'For the purposes of this Federal Act, missionary activity is defined as the activity of a religious association aimed at the dissemination of information about its creed among persons who are not participants (members, followers) of this religious association, in order to draw these persons as new participants (members, followers) of this religious association. It is carried out directly by religious associations or by authorised citizens, and/or legal entities in public, via mass media, information and telecommunication networks, the internet or other legal means.' However, paragraph 3 of Article 24.1 imposes restrictions upon missionary activity in residential premises.

Classification of Real Estate Objects for Religious Purposes

The Russian Federation legislation in this field is not perfect. Among other things, the content of the concept of religious property, described in paragraph 1 of Article 2 of the Federal Act 'On Restitution of Religious Property in State or Municipal Ownership to Religious Organisations', can reasonably be said to suffer from incompleteness and certain fragmentation.

Note that this study is limited exclusively to real estate objects for religious purposes and religious movable property. Objects of decor in religious buildings and structures, objects intended for worship and other religious purposes have not been considered. Obviously, there are no less issues in the field of religious movable property than in the theoretical and applied fields under study. It would be extremely difficult to study them because of the huge variety and significant heterogeneity of movable property, even when only a few major confessions are considered. As part of the study of the features and legal status of solely real estate objects for religious purposes, a huge variety and difference in the nature of these objects - from classical church buildings to 'sacred groves' of believers of certain religions in the Russian Far East and other regions across the world - have already been dealt with.

The following should be reasonably considered as the types of real estate objects for religious purposes[5]:

---

[5] Isidor, Metropolitan of Smolensk and Dorogobuzh (Tupikin R.V.) Real estate objects for religious purposes: Experience of Foreign Regulation / Edited by M.N. Kuznetsov / Institute of relations between the State and religious denominations and Law. – Smolensk: Svitok, 2019. – 320 p. – P. 46-48. Isidor, Metropolitan of Smolensk and Dorogobuzh (Tupikin R.V.) Civil Law and Contract Regulation of Property Relations of Religious Organisations in Foreign Countries / Edited by M.N. Kuznetsov / Institute of relations between the State and religious denominations and Law. – Moscow: Buki Vedi, 2016. – 179 p. Bagan V.V. Real Estate for Religious Purposes: Civil-legal Point of View / Edited by M.N. Kuznetsov / Institute of relations between the State and religious denominations and Law. – Moscow: Buki Vedi, 2017. – 208 p.; Bagan V.V. Legal Regime of Real Estate for Religious Purposes of the Russian Orthodox Church: Thesis for PhD (Law) / RUDN University. – Moscow, 2017. – 225 p.

- Ordinary (separate) property (buildings and structures) of religious worship function (religious buildings - a temple, a mosque, etc.; religious structures - a chapel, a worship cross installed on the land plot, etc.) with associated land plots (for example, in the city there are stand-alone temple buildings surrounded by residential, commercial, or industrial buildings), including those ruined and/or temporarily unused for their original purposes.

- Ordinary buildings with no direct religious worship function, which are used to support religious and associated activities of religious organisations (in accordance with Articles 6, 8, 5, 16, 18, 19, 21, 21.1 of Federal Act 'On the Freedom of Conscience and Religious Associations'), objects of industrial, social, charitable, cultural, educational, and other functions.

- Complex religious property (unified complex property groups), including not only religious buildings (places of worship, i.e. temples, mosques, etc.) with associated land plots, but also buildings supporting the activities (not only religious) of religious organisations: household buildings, buildings of educational organisations (buildings intended and/or used for educational and religious educational activities of religious organisations or related organisations), and buildings used for social work, together with the land under them and adjacent land plots (monastery complexes, temple complexes).

- Land plots on which previously standing religious buildings were not preserved (including those that were destroyed by the state), but the plots themselves remained religiously revered by believers, as well as undeveloped plots of land historically directly associated with religious rites or as places of religious pilgrimage.

- Confessional (religious) cemeteries, confessional sections of common cemeteries, religious buildings in such cemeteries or cemetery sections; burial places of religiously revered or highly respected believers.

- Cenotaphs with pronounced symbols or attributes of religious content on the roadside lanes of highways.
- Stand-alone worship crosses and chapels.
- Other material objects of a religious function, religiously venerated by believers and/or being places of religious pilgrimage or directly related to religious rites.
- The attribution of confessional cemeteries and confessional sections of common cemeteries to real estate objects for religious purposes is determined by the following circumstances:
- The nature and original purpose of religious (confessional) cemeteries and confessional sections of common cemeteries, which is expressed by the intention to turn such places into a homogeneous religious and cultural memorial, in their bond with religious secret.
- The imperative of legal support and protection of the human dignity of the deceased, through the recognition of a posthumous will (expressed during their life or presumed, based on their expressed belonging or preferential attitude to a particular religion) regarding a certain religious tradition, including the traditions regarding burial after death.
- The imperative of legal support and protection of human dignity of persons expressing religious veneration or respect for the deceased buried in such a cemetery, religious feelings of people for whom the obligation to respect the religious significance of such cemeteries is normatively established.
- The immanent conjugation of religious (confessional) cemeteries and confessional sections of common cemeteries with the implementation of acts of religious respect (and even veneration) and the conduct of religious rites (worship).

- The availability of religious buildings in religious (confessional) cemeteries and confessional sections of common cemeteries.

A difficult case is also worth mentioning regarding such an object of religious function as 'an apartment in which a revered religious ascetic, a spiritual master, lived which, as a result, became an object of veneration and pilgrimage but does not fit the definition of a religious site', which *de facto* became one, or 'a premise in the long-term possession of a religious association in which, as a result of its use, certain sacred events occurred that made the premise itself an object of religious veneration, which *de facto* became one of the objects of religious function'. This issue is quite common in Russia where, in 1917-1930 and later, numerous sites of real estate objects for religious purposes were subjected to destruction and, therefore, such a critical shortcoming occurred. The legislation of the Russian Federation in relation to such specific objects suffers from uncertainty and legal gaps, as well as some inconsistency.

Defects and Other Shortcomings of the Legislation of the Russian Federation in this Area

Specific religious property objects such as worship crosses, cenotaphs with religious symbols on roadside lanes, religious (confessional) cemeteries and confessional sections of common cemeteries, as well as unified groups of real estate objects for religious purposes (as complex objects) - monastery, temple and other complexes - have the most difficult and ambiguous legal status. The legal status of worship crosses (as specific religious property) and cenotaphs with religious symbols on roadside lanes as specific religious objects is uncertain; such objects fall simultaneously under intersectional and combinatorial regulation of several different legal regimes, while the specification of the legal status of such objects is very accidental.[6]

Another shortcoming of the legal regulation in this field is an obvious redundancy of normative legal regulation in the field of the restitution of religious property by the state or municipalities to religious organisations at the level of the constituent entities of the Russian Federation and at the level of municipalities. Such redundancy is not justified by the legal and factual specifics of the subject-object field.

According to the meaning of paragraph 3 of Article 21 of the Federal Act 'On the Freedom of Conscience and Religious Associations', the scope of the religious property concept is wider than only those of religious buildings and structures, even with the land plots related to them. Indeed, the concept of religious buildings and structures also has no clearly defined scope. The assumption can be made that the indicated norm also provides for religious movable property, which is fair, but the scope of real estate objects for religious purposes complexes is also not limited to religious buildings and structures, at least when relying on an interpretation of the concept of religious activities specified in paragraph 1 of Article 6, paragraph 1 of Article 7, and paragraph 1 of Article 8 of the Federal Act 'On the Freedom of Conscience and Religious Associations'.

Moreover, paragraph 5 of Article 21 and paragraph 2 of Article 21.1 also speak of the concept of 'real estate objects for worship purposes', without correlating them with the concept of 'religious buildings and structures', although in the second case, it is presumed that this concept is broader and includes the concept of 'real estate objects for worship purposes'.

There are a number of other defects in the legislation in this area.

---

[6] Bagan V.V. Legal Regime of Real Estate for Religious Purposes of the Russian Orthodox Church: Thesis for PhD (Law) / RUDN University. – Moscow, 2017. – 225pp., p. 14–15.

However, one cannot say that everything is bad. Russian legislation in this area fulfils its function. Although, the recent events related to the pandemic have posed many new problems for the legislation.

7

TURKEY

Assoc. Professor Dr Yannis Ktistakis, Ecumenical Patriarchate

The principle of secularism is heavily present both in letter and spirit within the Turkish constitutional text. Its presence can clearly be observed in the Preamble of the Constitution of 1982. It recognises that, 'no protection shall be accorded to an activity contrary to ... the nationalism, principles, reforms and modernism of Ataturk and, as required by the principle of secularism' and clearly states that 'there shall be no interference whatsoever by sacred religious feelings in state affairs and politics' (§5).

As a Republic, the Turkish State is a 'secular state ... based on the fundamental tenets set forth in the Preamble' (article 2). Moreover, within the context of the 'Irrevocable Provisions' regime set forth in article 4 of the Constitution, 'the provision of Article 1 of the Constitution establishing the form of the state as a Republic, the provisions in Article 2 on the characteristics of the Republic ... shall not be amended, nor shall their amendment be proposed'. In this respect, the principle of secularism, separating all religious aspects of life from state governance, is afforded legal safeguard against any constitutional initiatives that might aspire to distort its presence within the text.

The Turkish Constitution also foresees a self-preservation clause in article 174, with the essential intent of protecting legislation in force which substantiated *in concreto* the principle of secularism and the Reform Laws. Under article 174, 'No provision of the Constitution shall be construed or interpreted as rendering unconstitutional the Reform Laws indicated below, which aim to raise Turkish society above the level of contemporary civilization and to safeguard the secular character of the Republic, and whose provisions were in force on the date of the adoption of the Constitution by referendum'.

The laws and principles that are afforded under article 174 is, *inter alia*, the law on the Closure of Dervish Monasteries and Tombs.

Religious freedom itself is set forth clearly and comprehensively in article 24 of the Turkish Constitution entitled 'Freedom of Religion and Conscience', foreseeing both the individual freedom and safeguards against potential clashes with the principal of secularism. According to the article:

- Everyone has the right to freedom of conscience, religious belief and conviction.
- Acts of worship, religious services, and ceremonies shall be conducted freely, provided they do not violate the provisions of Article 14.[1]
- No one shall be compelled to worship, to participate in religious ceremonies and rites, to reveal religious beliefs and convictions, or be blamed or accused because of their religious beliefs and convictions.
- Education and instruction in religion and ethics shall be conducted under state supervision and control. Instruction in religious culture and moral education shall be compulsory in the curricula of primary and secondary schools. Other religious education and instruction shall be subject to the individual's own desire, and, in the case of minors, at the request of their legal representatives.

---

[1] Article 14 of the Constitution provides that none of the rights and freedoms in the Constitution shall be exercised in the form of activities aiming to eliminate the secular order of the Republic based on human rights.

- No one shall be allowed to exploit or abuse religion or religious feelings or things held sacred by religion in any manner whatsoever, for the purpose of personal or political influence, or for even partially basing the fundamental, social, economic, political, and legal order of the state on religious tenets.

Under article 90 of the Constitution, which regulates the status of international treaties in domestic law, the international agreements which Turkey is party to are superior to national law; when there are contradictions between the international agreements and national laws concerning human rights, the provisions of international conventions prevail. Accordingly, Turkey is party to two important human rights conventions which guarantee the right to freedom of thought, religion or belief, the United Nations International Covenant on Civil and Political Rights (ICCPR – articles 18 & 27)[2] and the European Convention of Human Rights (ECHR – article 9)[3].

However, according to the Turkish interpretation of secularism, the state has pervasive control over religion and denies full legal status to all religious communities. This limits religious freedom for all religious groups and has been particularly detrimental to the smallest minority faiths,[4] despite the fact that the non-discrimination clause also has constitutional protection.[5.]

---

[2] The International Covenant on Civil and Political Rights entered into force on 23 September 2003 in Turkey.

[3] The European Convention on Human Rights entered into force on 18 May 1954 in Turkey.

[4] Nominally, 99.0% of the Turkish population is Muslim, of whom a majority belong to the Sunni Branch of Islam. A sizeable minority of the population (10%-30%) is affiliated with the Alevi sect. The fewer than 150,000 Christians in Turkey include Armenian and Greek Orthodox, Bulgarian Orthodox, Maronite, Chaldean, Nestorian Assyrian and Roman Catholic communities. The Jew-

Within this framework, official control of Islam is construed according to article 136 of the Constitution through the Presidency of Religious Affairs:

'The Presidency of Religious Affairs, which is within the general administration, shall exercise its duties prescribed in its particular law, in accordance with the principles of secularism, removed from all political views and ideas, and aiming at national solidarity and integrity.'

Additionally, official control of all other faiths is through the Directorate-General for Foundations, which is under the President of the Republic (article 108 of the Constitution). More specifically, until recently (Law no. 5737/2008), the only form of legal entity open to religious communities was for its members to establish foundations, or by owning the property of the community (mosques, churches, schools, other auxiliary buildings etc.). The foundation system is old and dates to the Ottoman era tradition of *vakifs*, which is still its Turkish name. Almost all the foundations of the Greek Orthodox, Armenian and Jewish communities, as well as those of several others, date to before the 1923 establishment of the Turkish Republic, or at least back to the important 1936 registration of foundations (see below, §7). This applies to all foundations in Turkey, of which there are a great variety, with foundations having a direct or indirect relationship to religious activity being in the minority. All foundations are under the supervision of the Directorate-General for Foundations. For religious communities, the foundation system seems primarily to

---

ish community comprises fewer than 20,000 persons. Other smaller communities exist in Turkey, including Baha'is.

[5] Article 10 provides, inter alia, that 'everyone is equal before the law without distinction as to language, race, color, sex, political opinion, philosophical belief, religion and sect, or any such grounds'.

provide them with an indirect arrangement for property ownership and the financing of related religious activities.

Historically, the Turkish government expropriated (without remuneration) properties belonging to minority religious, in particular places of worship.

Most significant is the case of the so-called 'Autocephalous Turkish Orthodox Patriarchate', founded in Kayseri in 1922 by priest Efthim Karahisaritis, who was called Pope Efthim I. The legal basis of this foundation was a Council of Ministers' Decree of the Ankara government in 1921, during the occupation of Anatolia. When Orthodox people left Capadoccia in 1923 during the Population Exchange, the patriarchate, which no longer had a community, was moved to Istanbul in 1924 following another government decision. Papa Efthim and his family were exempt from the Population Exchange and were allowed to settle in Istanbul. Efthim changed his Greek name to Zeki Erenerol, confiscated the Phanar Church in Galata and declared himself a patriarch. Erenerol was excommunicated by the Ecumenical Patriarch on 19 February 1924. Later in 1965, he confiscated the Ayios Ioannis and Ayios Nikolaos churches in Galata, and registered these churches under the name of the Foundation for the Turkish Orthodox Church with the consent of the state, thus confiscating churches of the Ecumenical Patriarchate *de jure* and *de facto*. Upon Zeki Erenerol's death in 1968, he was succeeded by his sons and grandchildren. This church has not had any followers since 1968 and has not been recognised by any church. It never met the minimum requirements as an Orthodox church, did not follow the rules of the Greek Orthodox religion and only remained as an instrument used by the Turkish State to undermine the Ecumenical Patriarchate.[6]

Another significant case is the closure of the Grand Synagogue of Edirne (Kahal Kadosh ha Gadol). It was one of the synagogues built by

---

[6] Elçin Macar, Cumhuriyet Döneminde İstanb l Rum Patrikhanesi (Greek Patriarchate in Istanbul during the Republican Era), İ etişi , 2004.

imperial order of Sultan Abdü'hamit II after a fire destroyed several synagogues in 1905. It was left to disrepair after the Jewish community, approximately 20,000 people, was forced to flee Edirne as a result of threats and attacks against the Jews of the region in 1934. The Foundation of the Grand Synagogue of Edirne was taken over by the Directorate-General of Foundations in 1995 for 'no longer having any humanitarian or practical value'. The Foundation of the Grand Synagogue of Edirne and the synagogue itself are currently under the administration of the Directorate-General for Foundations (a fused foundation).

The practice of fused foundations, *mazbut vakıf,* is the principal way the Directorate-General for Foundations has restricted the freedom of worship. It takes over the management of foundations deemed to 'no longer be of charitable or practical use'.[7] Through this practice, the Directorate General for Foundations particularly targeted foundations that lost their communities over time due to the sharp decline in the non-Muslim population in Turkey since the 1960s. The migration (forced or otherwise) of non-Muslims has left the vast majority of their churches non-functioning. Instead of allowing non-Muslim communities to make use of their real estate in other ways based on their needs and preferences, the Turkish state seized control of the foundations responsible for running these institutions. Since the 1960s, the Directorate General for Foundations has seized nineteen Greek Orthodox foundations[8] and

---

[7] According to article 3 of Law 5737/2008, 'Fused (Mazbut) Foundations refer to those ones to be administered and represented by the Directorate General under this Law [no. 5737/2008], and those ones which were founded before the enforcement date of the abolished Turkish Civil Law no. 743/1926 and are administered by the General Directorate of Foundations in accordance with the Foundations Law no. 2762/1935'. In other words, Fused (Mazbut) Foundations maintain their individual legal existence. They are in a sense 'partially incapable' legal entities.

[8] Burgazada Hristos Greek Monastery, Büyüka a Aya Nikola Greek Monastery, Büyüka a Aya Yorgi (Koudouna) Greek Monastery, Büyü' ada Hristos Greek

twenty-four Jewish foundations, taking over their management and confiscating their respective churches and synagogues.[9]

Moreover, concerning the religious foundations not seized, the Directorate General for Foundations has continued seizure policies. In 2013, it cancelled the existing regulation on election procedures for the management board of non-Muslim foundations, without replacing it with another. Since 2013, there continues to be no regulation and this continues to prevent minority religious foundations from electing board members. The minority representative on the Foundations Council in the Directorate General for Foundations resigned in 2014 over the lack of legal framework allowing religious foundations to elect its management boards.[10]

In addition, through the Land Registry legislation, the Directorate-General for Foundations has also restricted minorities' freedom of worship. Foundations law no. 2762/1935 recognised the legal personality of Greek Orthodox, Armenians and Jewish foundations set up under the Ottoman Empire. This law imposed an obligation for minority foundations, created under the Ottoman Empire, to submit a declaration indicating the nature and amount of their income among other things. All the

---

Monastery, Vefa Panayia Church and Holy Spring, Edirnekapı Aya Yorgi Greek Orthodox Church, Kınalıada Hristos Greek Monastery, İsti ye Taksiarhi Greek Orthodox Church, Gökçeada Aya Marina Kaleköy Church, Gökçeada Aya Varvara Greek Church, Heybeliada Aya Spiridon Monastery, Heybeliada Hristos Monastery, Fener Agios Georgios Potiras Church, Tarabya Aya Yorgi Greek Church, Salkımsöğü' Aya Terapi Holy Spring (Ayiasma Ag. Therapontos), Aya Yani Church and Monastery of St Catherine of Sinai Great Monastery, Heybeliada Aya Yorgi Greek Monastery of the Patriarchate of Jerusalem, Fener Aya Giorgi Church of the Patriarchate of Jerusalem and Doka Veledi Petro Sofyanos Tahta Minare District Foundation of the Patriarchate of Jerusalem.

[9] A full list of fused churches and synagogues in: Dilek Kurban & Konstantinos Tsitselikis, A Tale of Reciprocity: Minority Foundations in Greece and Turkey, Tesev, 2010, p. 36-37.

[10] European Commission, Turkey Progress Report, October 2014, p. 56.

minority foundations submitted the declaration, Declarations 1936, indicating immovable property and places of worship.

In the case-law established by its judgment of 8 May 1974, the Turkish Court of Cassation decided that the Declarations of 1936 were to be regarded as the constitutive instruments of the foundations, finalising their constitutions. Unless the Declaration 1936 included an express provision to such effect, foundations were not entitled to acquire immovable property other than that declared in the said document. The Court of Cassation appeared to consider that the acquisition by foundations of this type of property, in addition to that which was indicated in their constitution, could present a threat to national security.

With the 1974 Court of Cassation judgment, immovable taken by community foundations with endowment, legacy and purchase between 1936-1974, were returned to their ex-tenants and some of these properties were assigned to State Treasury, Directorate General of Foundations or third persons.

The legislation that governed foundations was finally changed in 2002 under Section 4 of Law no. 4771/2002, which for the first time provided that religious community foundations were entitled to acquire and alienate immovable property, whether or not they had a constitutive instrument.[11] A year later, under pressure from the European Union, an administrative procedure was provided for the restitution of confiscated immovable properties of religious foundations since 1936, also for the first time. Later, the 2008 Law on Foundations (no. 5737) provided a broadened administrative procedure for the restitution of confiscated properties, which finalised, on the third attempt, the procedure launched on 2011. Nevertheless, Turkish legislation did not cover fused religious foundations and properties of foundations transferred to third persons. Under this legislation, 116 minority community foundations applied for

---

[11] ECtHR, Fener Rum Erkek Lisesi Vakfı v. Turkey, no. 34478/97, 9.1.2007, §§ 23-30.

the restitution of a total of 1560 properties. The Foundations Council approved the return of 333 properties and compensation for twenty-one properties. 1206 applications were found to be ineligible.[12]

Some of the above property claims have been examined by the European Court of Human Rights in Strasbourg. In the case Bozcaada Kimisis Teodoku Rum Ortodoks Kilisesi Vakfi (no. 2), concerning the refusal to enter Greek Orthodox Church foundation in land registers as owners of property, the European Court of Human Rights (ECtHR) held that the restriction of property rights was incompatible with the principle of legality. In view of the specific characteristics of the properties, comprised of a Greek Orthodox community cemetery, a Greek Orthodox chapel and a former Greek Orthodox monastery, the Court considered that the restitution of the properties in question and their entry in the land registry in the applicant's name constituted the only adequate means of redress.[13]

In the case Cumhuriyetçi Eğitim ve Kültür Merkezi Vakfı v. Turkey, the ECtHR found that the refusal by the Presidency of Religious Affairs to pay the electricity bills for an Alevi religious centre housing a *cemevi* (an Alevi place of worship) in the same way it paid energy bills for mosques, churches and synagogues, violated both Article 14 of the ECHR, prohibition of discrimination, and Article 9 protecting freedom of belief. This refusal was based on the non-recognition of a *cemevi* as a place of worship, which was, in turn, the result of the Turkish authorities' refusal to consider Alevism as a separate religion rather than as a

---

[12] European Commission, Turkey Progress Reports, October 2014 (p. 16) and November 2016 (p. 74). See also, the relevant State information (Directorate General of Foundations): https://www.vgm.gov.tr/foundations-in-turkey/foundations-in-turkey/cemaat-community-foundations

[13] ECtHR, Bozcaada Kimisis Teodoku Rum Ortodoks Kilisesi Vakfi (no. 2) v. Turkey, 6.10.2009, nos. 37646/03, 37665/03, 37992/03, 37993/03 & 37996/03.

branch of Islam.[14] Following the ECtHR judgment, the Assembly of Civil Chambers of the Turkish Court of Appeals ruled that the status of *cemevis* as places of worship was not something that could be determined by a court decision.[15]

Finally, the ECtHR found a violation of freedom of worship in a case concerning the closing of private premises previously used by two congregations of Turkish Jehovah's Witnesses, on the basis of a law prohibiting the opening of places of worship on sites not set aside for that purpose, and the subsequent dismissal of their requests to use those premises as places of worship. In this case the congregations were also informed that the local urban development plans did not include any suitable site for a place of worship. The Court noted that the domestic authorities had not considered the specific needs of a small community of believers, as the limited number of adherents meant that the congregations in question needed a simple meeting room where they could hold their services, meet and teach their religion, rather than a building with a specific type of architecture.[16]

Many places of worship around Turkey currently face destruction or are disappearing. Such places are important for the religious or belief communities. For example, the St. George Armenian Church in Mardin, known locally as the Red Church, was included in 'Europe's Seven Most Endangered' cultural sites program (Europa Nostra Turkey). After 1915, this building was never used as a church again and served as an orphanage and as a barrack. While its property rights belong to the Mardin Armenian Catholic Church Community Foundation, it does not appear possible for the foundation to collect the necessary budget for the

---

[14] Cumhuriyetçi Eğitim ve Kültü Merkezi Vakfı v. Turkey, 2.12.2014, 32093/10.

[15] Court of Cassation General Assembly, 31.12.2014, E/ 2014/7-1038 K/2014/990.

[16] Association for Solidarity with Jehovah's Witnesses and Others v. Turkey, 36915/10 & 8606/13, 24.5.2016.

church's restoration, nor does it receive financial support from the Ministry of Culture or the Directorate General of Foundations. The church foundation seeks not only to restore the church but to use is for worship services as well.

Nevertheless, some notable non-Muslim places of worship owned by the government were restored, having been characterised as historical monuments. The 1100-year-old Akdamar Armenian Orthodox Church was renovated in 2007. The Bulgarian Church of Sveti Stefan, also known as the Iron Church, is the world's only surviving entirely iron church, and dates to the 19th century. The church was damaged over time and was restored by the government between 2011 and 2017.

In June 2010, the Turkish State allowed the Ecumenical Patriarchate to hold a divine liturgy to mark the Feast of the Assumption on 15 August 2010, in the Panagia Sumela Monastery (Trabzon). It was the first time in eighty-eight years that the monastery was reopened as a church, having been converted into a museum in previous years. Sümela Monaster was once again closed in 2015 for restoration to dismantle danger caused by the rock masses around Karadağ Mountain. Restoration works have also been ongoing inside the historical monastery.

More recently, Turkey's Council of State, the country's highest administrative court, has approved changing the historic Chora Greek Orthodox Church, located in Istanbul and currently a museum, into a mosque. The church was transformed into a mosque under the Ottoman Empire and in 1945 the building was again transformed, this time to the Kariye Museum. However, a lawsuit filed in 2005 by the Association of Permanent Foundations and Service to Historical Artifacts and Environment challenged this decision. They claimed that, as a mosque, it is a public immovable belonging to the Fatih Sultan Mehmet Foundation. The 2019 decision by the Council of State affirms this belief:

'The Kariye mosque... is one of the public immovables belonging to the Fatih Sultan Mehmet Foundation... Immovables are public property established for direct charitable services such as places of worship, hospitals, and soup kitchens, and the provisions of private property cannot be applied to them. These charitable public immovables cannot be allocated to be used for a purpose other than the use specified by the [Fatih sultan Mehmet] Foundation'.

8

PROTECTION
UNDER INTERNATIONAL LAW:
UN/EU FRAMEWORK

Assoc. Professor Dr Yannis Ktistakis, Ecumenical Patriarchate

Religious freedom, protecting the individual and his beliefs, either alone or in community with others, in a general and systematic way, constitutes one of individual's rights that particularly aims at maintaining the peaceful character of modern society. The international community, fully aware of this particularity of religious freedom, wished to secure it more efficiently after the end of World War II than in the past. Article 18 of the Universal Declaration on Human Rights (Universal Declaration),[1] Article 18 of the International Covenant on Civil and Political Rights (ICCPR)[2] and the Declaration on the Elimination of all Forms of Intolerance and of Discrimination based on Religion or Belief, safeguard, above all, religious freedom (the 1981 Declaration).[3]

The protection of religious freedom has long been indispensable for the peaceful coexistence of peoples, especially in Europe. Following bitter experiences of religious disputes from the distant past, at the end of

---

[1] Adopted by General Assembly of UN, Resolution 217 A(III) of 10 December 1948.

[2] UN, New York, 16.12.1966, UNTS, T. 999, p. 171.

[3] Proclaimed by the UN General Assembly, Resolution 36/55 of 25 November 1981.

the World War II, European states wanted to safeguard religious freedom in two ways. Firstly, they included it again in all their post-war Constitutions without exception and, secondly, they introduced it to the new European Convention for the Protection of Human Rights and Fundamental Freedoms (ECHR), which was signed in 1950 and started to come into force in the various member states.[4]

Recently, the European Union has given legal basis to the Charter of Fundamental Rights,[5] proclaimed in 2000, which also protects freedom of thought, conscience and religion in the same way as the Convention (Article 10 of the Charter).[6]

Since 1993, the number of cases examined by the European Court of Human Rights (ECtHR) has constantly been increasing under article 9 of the ECHR (Freedom of Thought, Conscience and Religion). This trend can be explained by the increasing importance of religion and related matters in European socio-political discourse after the fall of Berlin wall. It can also be explained by the fact that the ECHR is the only legally binding text that actually provides judicial control of forty-seven European states in the field of human rights, namely by a special international supervisory judicial body, the well-known ECtHR, established in 1959.

---

[4] CoE, Rome, 4.11.1950, UNTS, t. 213, p.221 / ETS, no. 5.

[5] Treaty of Lisbon amending the Treaty on European Union and the Treaty establishing the European Community (OJ C 306, 17.12.2007); entry into force on 1 December 2009.

[6] According to the explanations, originally prepared under the authority of the Praesidium of the Convention which drafted the Charter of Fundamental Rights of the European Union (see the Preamble of the Charter), 'the right guaranteed in paragraph 1 of Article 10 corresponds to the right guaranteed in Article 9 of the ECHR and, in accordance with article 52(3) of the Charter, has the same meaning and scope. Limitations must therefore respect Article 9(2) of the ECHR'.

The wording of Article 9 of the ECHR distinguishes two fields of protection: *forum internum* and *forum externum*. The first field (internal dimension) enjoys absolute protection. The second field (external dimension) is subject to the limitations of the article 9(2):

- Everyone has the right to freedom of thought, conscience and religion; this right includes freedom to change religion or belief and freedom, either alone or in community with others and in public or private, to manifest their religion or belief, in worship, teaching, practice and observance.

- Freedom to manifest one's religion or beliefs shall be subject only to such limitations as prescribed by law and are necessary in a democratic society in the interests of public safety, for the protection of public order, health or morals, or for the protection of the rights and freedoms of others.

As opposed to what applies to *forum internum*, the text contains a detailed list of the various forms of manifesting religious beliefs[7] in worship, in observance, in practice and in teaching.[8]

The content of worship in the ECHR is neither broad nor clear, which is due to its semantic connection with observance. The Human Rights Committee, interpreting the corresponding article 18 of the ICCPR, clarified that the meaning of worship includes 'the ceremonial and typical acts that constitute a straight expression of beliefs, as well as practices that are inseparable from the devotional and ceremonial acts, including the construction of worship places, the use of devotional types

---

[7] The ways of manifesting religious beliefs are mentioned in article 9(1) ECHR, in pairs and exhaustively: either alone or in community with others, in public or private (ECtHR, X v. the United Kingdom, 8160/78, Commission (Decision), 12.3.1981 · ECtHR, Masaev v. Moldova, 6303/05, 12.5.2009, §§ 22-26).

[8] ECtHR, Güle and Uğur v. Turkey, 31706/10 & 33088/10, 2.12.2014, § 35.

and objects, the presentation of symbols and the devotional practice during feasts and holidays'.[9]

Undoubtedly, article 9 includes the right to operate[10] and maintain[11] places of worship as being the temple[12] (or hall[13] or apartment[14] or complex of buildings[15]), the offices of the temple[16] and the cemetery[17]. On the contrary, the general immovable property of the religious community is not considered to be destined for the furtherance of devotional needs, even if this property is administered by religious organs.[18] Article 9 does not grant a religious community the right to obtain a place of worship from the public authorities.[19] The mere fact that the public au-

---

[9] Human Rights Committee, General Comment no. 22, CCPR/C/21/ Rev.1/ Add.4, 27.9.1993, § 4.

[10] ECtHR, Association Les Témoins de Jéhovah v. France, 8916/05, 30.6.2011, § 53 · ECtHR, Association for Solidarity with Jehovah's Witnesses and Others v. Turkey, 36915/10 & 8606/13, 24.5.2016, §§ 90 & 107.

[11] ECtHR, Church of Jesus Christ of Latter-Day Saints v. the United Kingdom, 7552/09, 4.3.2014, § 30 · ECtHR, Cumhuriyetçi Eğitim ve Kü'tüï erkezi Vakfı v. Turkey, 2.12.2014, 32093/10, § 41.

[12] ECtHR, Gromada Ukrayinskoyi Greko-Katolytskoyi Tserkvy Sela Korshiv v. Ukraine, 9557/04, 3.5.2016, §§ 4, 36 & 37.

[13] ECtHR, Manoussakis and others, 18748/91, 26.9.1996, § 7.

[14] ECtHR, Tanyar and others v. Turkey, 74242/01, Decision, 7.6.2005.

[15] ECtHR, Association Les Témoins de Jéhovah v. France, 8916/05, 30.6.2011, § 8 & 53.

[16] ECtHR, Serbisch-Griechisch-Orientalische Kirchengemeinde Zum Helligen Sava in Wien v. Austria, 13712/88, Commission (Decision), 2.4.1990.

[17] ECtHR, Johannische Kirche & Horst Peters v. Germany, 41754/98, 17.7.2001.

[18] ECtHR, The Holy Monasteries v. Greece, 13092/87 & 13984/88, 9.12.1994, § 86 ECtHR, Institut de Prêtres Français and others v. Turkey, 26308/95, Commission (Decision), 19.1.1998.

[19] ECtHR, Association for Solidarity with Jehovah's Witnesses and Others v. Turkey, 36915/10 & 8606/13, 24.5.2016, § 97 ECtHR, Griechische Kirchengemeinde Munchen und Bayern E.V. v. Germany, 52336/99, Decision, 18.9.2007.

thorities have tolerated the continued use of a state-owned building for religious purposes for a number of years gives rise to no positive obligation on the part of those authorities.[20] Article 9 does not, as such, afford a religious community any right to the return of the ownership of a building of worship long confiscated (in the 1930s, in the case at hand) by the political regime of the time.[21] Nor do the provisions of the Convention imply any obligation by the state to grant special status to places of worship. Nevertheless, if the state itself offers special privileged status to places of worship – above and beyond its obligations under the Convention – it cannot deny this advantage to specified religious groups in a discriminatory manner contrary to Article 14 ECHR.[22]

Freedom of worship is not unlimited. The first decision on Article 9 before the ECtHR already ruled that 'within a democratic society, where many religions coexist in the same population, it may be necessary to impose restrictions on this freedom in order to harmonise the interests of different groups and to ensure that everyone's beliefs are respected'.[23] Religious freedom is subject to general (Article 15 ECHR) and special restrictions. The limitations of the second paragraph of Article 9, which are intended to protect the public and private interests and concern exclusively the right to the manifestation of beliefs, are special. In order for special restrictions to be justified, they must a) be provided for by law, b) serve a legitimate purpose (public safety, protection of public order, health, morals and protection of the rights and freedoms of others), and c) be necessary in a democratic society. According to case-law, 'provided by law' means that the impugned measure should have a legal

---

[20] ECtHR, Juma Mosque Congregation and others v. Azerbaijan, 15405/04, 8.1.2013, § 60.

[21] ECtHR, Rymsko-Katolytska Gromada Svyatogo Klymentiya v. Misti Sevastopoli v. Ukraine, 22607/02, 3.5.2016, §§ 59-63.

[22] ECtHR, Cumhuriyetçi Eğitim ve Kültü" Merkezi Vakfı v. Turkey, 2.12.2014, 32093/10, § 48.

[23] ECtHR, Kokkinakis v. Greece, 14307/88, 25.5.1993, § 33.

basis on domestic law,[24] the relevant law should be accessible to the interested person,[25] who should also be capable of foreseeing the consequences, and for that[26] the law should be compatible with the principle of rule of law.[27] Moreover, the court examines, under the condition of 'necessary in a democratic society', a) the necessity of the restrictive measure, b) the consistency of the measure with a democratic society, and c) the proportionality of the measure as a means of attaining the legitimate aim.

In application of the above standards, the ECtHR has examined several cases concerning, inter alia, Greece, Turkey, Germany, United Kingdom, Austria, Switzerland, France and Azerbaijan in the field of freedom of worship. Among the applicants were Jehovah's Witnesses, Greek Old Calendarists, Protestants and Muslims.

In the famous Manoussakis and Others case, the applicants were sentenced to a prison term and a fine for using a private room rented to serve as a place of worship for the Jehovah's Witnesses without having obtained prior authorisation from the 'recognised ecclesiastical authori-

---

[24] ECtHR, Igors Dmitrijevs c. Lettonie, 61638/00, 30.11.2006, §§ 79-80 · ECtHR, Moroz v. Ukraine, 5187/07, 2.3.2017, §§ 105-107 · ECtHR, Dogru v. France, 27058/05, 4.1.2008, § 52 · ECtHR, Ebrahimian v. France, 64846/11, 26.11.2015, § 48 · ECtHR, Kervanci c. France, 31645/04, 4.1.2008, § 59 ECtHR, Mockutė v. Lithuania, 66490/09, 27.2.2018, §§ 128-130.

[25] ECtHR, Poltoratskiy v. Ukraine, 38812/97, 29.4.2003, §§ 158 και 170 · ECtHR, Kuznetsov and Others v. Ukraine, 39042/97, 23.4.2003, §§ 138 και 150.

[26] ECtHR, Leyla Şahin v. Turkey, 44774/98, 10.11.2005 [GC], §§ 91 και 98 · ECtHR, Svyato-Mykhaylivska Parafiya v. Ukraine, 77703/01, 14.6.2007, § 102 · ECtHR, Leela Förderkreis E.V. and Others v. Germany, 58911/00, 6.11.2008, §§ 88-90 · ECtHR, Krupko and Others v. Russia, 26587/07, 26.6.2014, § 54 · ECtHR, Biblical Centre of the Chuvash Republic v. Russia, 33203/08, 12.6.2014, § 56.

[27] ECtHR, Hasan and Chaush v. Bulgaria, 30985/96, 28.10.2000 [GC], § 87 · ECtHR, Religious Community of Jehovah's Witnesses of Kryvyi Rih's Ternivsky District v. Ukraine, 21477/10, 3.9.2019, §§ 55 και 57.

ty' (i.e. the local Greek Orthodox bishop) and the Ministry of Education and Religious Affairs. The ECtHR found it violated Article 9 because the relevant provisions of domestic law conferred an exorbitant discretionary power on the authorities in this sphere, a power they used in practice to restrict the activities of denominations other than the dominant Orthodox Church.[28]

In another Greek case,[29] the local authorities dismissed an applicant's request to amend the local development plan in order to enable him to build a house of prayer for the 'True Orthodox Christians' (Greek Old Calendarists or *Paleoimerologites*) on a plot of land he owned. The reason given for this refusal was that there was no 'social need' to amend the development plan because the municipality had insufficient members of the religious community in question. The ECtHR found that, in contrast to the Manoussakis and Others case, this case concerned the application of a general spatial planning law which was, on the face of it, neutral. The quantitative criterion applied by the Greek Supreme Court could not be described as arbitrary because authorisation to amend the local development could only be granted for the construction of a building 'in the public interest'. In such a hypothesis, it was reasonable to take account of the objective needs of the religious community since the public interest in rational spatial planning could not be supplanted by the religious needs of one single person, whereas a neighbouring town comprised a house of prayer catering for the needs of the True Orthodox Christians in the region. Greece had, therefore, acted within the limits of its margin of appreciation and the ECtHR found no violation.

---

[28] ECtHR, Manoussakis and others v. Greece, 18748/91, 26.9.1996, § 48. See, also, ECtHR, Pentidis and others v. Greece, 23238/94, 9.6.1997 · ECtHR, Tsavachidis v. Greece, 28802/95, 21.1.1999 [GC] · ECtHR, Vergos v. Greece, 65501/01, 24.6.2004, § 34 · ECtHR, Miroļubovs and others v. Latvia, 798/05, 5.9.2009, § 90.

[29] ECtHR, Vergos v. Greece, 65501/01, 24.6.2004.

Following to Manoussakis and Others, the applicants in a Turkish case, members of a Protestant church, were sentenced to a fine for having used a private apartment which they had purchased as a place of worship, without having complied with the requisite formalities under Turkish law, especially the mandatory prior agreement of all the joint owners of the building. The ECtHR found that, unlike Manoussakis and Others, the formalities did not concern the recognition or the exercise of any religion and could not, therefore, be regarded as equivalent to prior authorisation. They were geared solely to protecting the rights and freedoms of others and public order. The ECtHR also noted that the national authorities had balanced compliance with the formalities in question with the requirements of freedom of religion by first inviting the applicants to comply with those formalities. As such, the impugned interference could be seen as justified and proportionate (no violation).[30]

Finally, the expulsion of a Muslim congregation from an old mosque building, listed as an historic monument in Azerbaijan, was examined by the ECtHR. Despite the applicant congregation using the building for more than ten years, it neither owned nor rented it, contrasting with the situation in the Manoussakis and Others case. In particular, the applicant congregation failed to argue that it was unable to freely set up a place of worship elsewhere. The ECtHR declared the application manifestly ill-founded.[31]

The ECtHR also considered an application from an individual under Articles 14 and 9 of the Convention concerning a ban on building minarets, which had been added to the Swiss Federal Constitution by referendum. It decided that, as the applicant was not directly affected by the impugned measure and had never personally voiced any wish to build a

---

[30] ECtHR, Tanyar and others v. Turkey, 74242/01, Decision, 7.6.2005.

[31] ECtHR, Juma Mosque Congregation and others v. Azerbaijan, 15405/04, Decision, 8.1.2013.

mosque with a minaret, he could not claim to be a victim of the alleged violation.[32]

The Association for Solidarity with Jehovah's Witnesses and Others case related to the closing of private premises previously used by two congregations of Turkish Jehovah's Witnesses on the basis of a law prohibiting the opening of places of worship on sites not set aside for that purpose, and the subsequent dismissal of their requests to use those premises as places of worship. In this case, the congregations were also informed that the local urban development plans did not include any suitable sites for a place of worship. The ECtHR noted that the domestic authorities had not considered the specific needs of a small community of believers, as the limited number of adherents meant that the congregations in question needed a simple meeting room where they could hold their services, meet and teach their religion, rather than a building with a specific type of architecture.[33]

In the Religious Community of Jehovah's Witnesses of Kryvyi Rih's Ternivsky District case, the applicant was unable to obtain a long-term lease on a plot of land belonging to an Ukrainian municipality, to erect a new Kingdom Hall (place of worship), despite the community already owning a building on that plot of land, which it used as a place of worship, and that all the formal conditions for allocating the land had been fulfilled. The restriction of the freedom of worship was ruled by the ECtHR as 'not prescribed by law' within the interpretation of Article 9 §2.[34]

The application Daratsakis v. Greece has been declared by the ECtHR as manifestly ill-founded. The application concerned a decision by

---

[32] ECtHR, Ouardiri v. Switzerland, 65840/09, Decision, 28.6.2011.

[33] ECtHR, Association for Solidarity with Jehovah's Witnesses and Others v. Turkey, 36915/10 & 8606/13, 24.5.2016.

[34] ECtHR, Religious Community of Jehovah's Witnesses of Kryvyi Rih's Ternivsky District v. Ukraine, 21477/10, 3.9.2019.

the Greek authorities to order an adherent of the Greek Orthodox Church to move his father's grave to facilitate road widening works. The ECtHR (European Commission of Human Rights) noted that other individuals of Orthodox religion in the same situation had voluntarily moved their family graves and that the Greek Orthodox Church authorities contacted by the applicant had refused to intervene in his favour. Moreover, according to the ECtHR, the applicant had not demonstrated how moving the grave would prevent him from discharging the duties prescribed by his beliefs or how the discharging of those duties would require the grave to remain in its original place.[35]

In a similar case, the German authorities refused to grant a permit to install a cemetery in an undeveloped protected zone to a religious organisation. The ECtHR held that the impugned interference, which had been based on legal provisions relating to planning, environmental conservation and the installation of public services, and had in particular been motivated by the fact that there were no other constructions in the zone in question, was in conformity with Article 9 §2.[36]

The ISKCON and Others v. the United Kingdom case related to a notice served by a local planning authority to the International Society for Krishna Consciousness Ltd. concerning the use of a manor purchased by that society and ordering it to restrict its use to that which had been authorised at the time of purchase (residential theological college and place of worship accommodating a maximum of one thousand visitors per day). In fact, the actual use of the manor for religious purposes had since greatly expanded, attracting large crowds leading to numerous complaints from neighbours. The ECtHR acknowledged that there had been an interference in the applicant society's exercise of freedom of religion but that such interference had been justified under Article 9 §2. In particular, it found that the local authorities had made constant efforts

---

[35] ECtHR, Daratsakis v. Greece, 12902/87, Commission (Decision), 7.10.1987.

[36] ECtHR, Johannische Kirche & Horst Peters v. Germany, 41754/98, 17.7.2001.

to reach a friendly settlement to the problem and that the applicant society's religious interest had been adequately taken into account in the domestic decision-making process. The ECtHR declared the application manifestly ill-founded.[37]

Finally, in an Austrian case, Serbisch-griechisch-orientalische Kirchengemeinde zum Heiligen Sava in Wien, the facts concerned the behaviour of the curator appointed by the Austrian courts to manage the property of a Serbian Orthodox community. Its power to act in the sphere of secular law had been suspended by law owing to the community's schismatic situation vis-à-vis the Belgrade Patriarchate. The curator had concluded tenancy contracts with two priests appointed by the Serbian Patriarch and the competent bishop. The ECtHR decided that the interference had been necessary for the protection of the rights of others and had been proportionate to that aim because the impugned measure had been limited in scope and the tenancy contracts would only remain valid as long as the schismatic situation lasted. The ECtHR declared the application manifestly ill-founded.[38]

---

[37] ECtHR, ISKCON and 8 Others v. the United Kingdom, 20490/92, Commission (Decision), 8.3.1994.

[38] ECtHR, Serbisch-Griechisch-Orientalische Kirchengemeinde Zum Helligen Sava in Wien v. Austria, 13712/88, Commission (Decision), 2.4.1990.

9

NON-TRADITIONAL SACRED SITES:
THE NEED FOR PROTECTION

Prof. Dr W. Cole Durham, Jr., BYU

Introduction

At the international level, substantial attention has been focused in recent years on the need for protection of heritage sites that have both historical and religious significance. Such sites can become linked to controversial issues of national identity or internal religious disputes over ownership of property. Tensions can arise between those interested in a site for use as a location of worship and those with a primarily historical or cultural interest. Problems may also arise due to shortfalls in funding for maintenance of historical structures, particularly where a structure has continued significance for worship and other religious uses, rights to freedom of religion or belief are almost certain to be involved. The international community may share any or all these interests and, like public authorities at the local and national levels, will in addition have an overriding interest in promoting just and peaceful resolution of conflicts.

This article addresses the core issue that arises in sacred site cases from the perspective of the relevant dimension of freedom of religion or belief (FoRB): the right to establish and maintain places of worship. The focus is not on the sites of dominant religions, which have typically played a major role in shaping national and cultural traditions, but on the sites of minority and non-traditional religions, and their struggle to establish, maintain and protect the sites that become sacred for their believers. The article first addresses the international norms that constitute the international framework for protecting such rights, and then discusses examples of the all too frequent cases, with an in-depth look at a set of cases from Russia, where the right to establish and maintain places of worship is violated and ignored. For most religious communities this right as it has been elaborated in international standard setting processes is critical to manifesting their religion. If this dimension of religious life is forgotten at the relatively mundane level of places of worship,[1] sacred heritage sites risk becoming little more than hollow museums of a dimly remembered past, rather than monuments of a still vibrant present. Care must be taken to assure that this critical dimension of freedom of religion or belief is not ignored. This is true both with respect to the rights of non-traditional religious communities, whose sacred space often goes unprotected, and with respect to the rights of more dominant religions, which are at risk of being prejudiced by well-intended efforts that place protection of heritage ahead of protecting core religious freedom rights.

---

* Susa Young Gates University Professor of Law, J. Reuben Clark Law School, Brigham Young University and Director, International Center for Law and Religion Studies at BYU. A.B., Harvard College, 1972; J.D. Harvard Law School, 1975. The author thanks Donlu Thayer for research and editorial assistance in preparation of this article, and also James Toronto, for collaboration on an earlier presentation that formed a basis for part of this article.[1] For a discussion of reasons to choose between the terminology of places of worship and sacred or holy sites, see Peter Petkoff, Finding a Grammar of Consent for 'Soft Law' Guidelines on Sacred Places: 'The Legal Protection of Sacred Places within the Existing Public International Law Instruments and Grass-Root Approaches', in Silvio Ferrari and Andrea Benzo (eds.), Between Cultural Diversity and Common Heritage (Ashgate 2014), 58.

The International Legal Framework for Protecting of the Right to Establish and Maintain Places of Worship

The right to establish and maintain places of worship is grounded in the broad protections of freedom of religion and belief provided by Article 18 of the Universal Declaration of Human Rights (UDHR)[2] and Article 18 of the International Covenant on Civil and Political Rights (ICCPR).[3] This right did not receive explicit mention, however, until adoption of the 1981 UN Declaration on the Elimination of All Forms of Intolerance and of Discrimination Based on Religion or Belief[4] (1981 Declaration). Article 6 of the 1981 Declaration provides in relevant part 'the right to freedom of thought, conscience, religion or belief shall include, inter alia, the following freedoms: ... (a) To worship or assemble in connection with a religion or belief and *to establish and maintain places for these purposes.*'[5] In general, Article 6 of the 1981 Declaration has particular significance because, whereas most of the Declaration's other articles simply repeat (almost verbatim) the binding but abstract treaty language of the ICCPR, Article 6 goes further and adds concreteness. Where the UDHR and the ICCPR define the entire range of manifestation of religion in terms of 'teaching, practice, worship, and observance',[6] Article 6 adds specificity to this condensed formula. In the words of Natan Lerner, a major expert on freedom of religion or belief,

---

[2] Universal Declaration on Human Rights (1948), GA Res. 217A(III), UN Doc. A/3/810 (1949).

[3] International Covenant on Civil and Political Rights (1966), 999 UNTS 171.

[4] Declaration on the Elimination of All Forms of Intolerance and of Discrimination Based on Religion or Belief (1981), GA Res. 36/55, UN Doc.A/36/51 (1982).

[5] 1981 Declaration, Article 6(a) (emphasis added).

[6] Paul Taylor, Freedom of Religion or Belief: Ensuring Effective International Legal Protection (The Hague, Boston, and London: Martinus Nijhoff Publishers, 2005), 22.

the concrete list of freedoms spelled out in Article 6 of the 1981 Declaration constitutes 'a detailed enunciation of rights belonging to the accepted minimum standard.'[7]

Further protection for religious sites has been vouchsafed by UN General Assembly Resolution 55/254, which called upon all states 'to exert their utmost efforts to ensure that religious sites are fully respected and protected' and 'to adopt adequate measures aimed at preventing such acts or threats of violence'.[8]

The link between the UDHR and ICCPR formulations of the right to freedom of religion or belief, and the more concrete right to establish and maintain places of worship, has been further attested by the UN Human Rights Committee, the body created pursuant to the ICCPR and formally charged with administering its provisions. In General Comment No. 22 to the ICCPR, the Committee affirmed that

> 'The freedom to manifest religion or belief in worship, observance, practice and teaching encompasses a broad range of acts. The concept of worship extends to ritual and ceremonial acts giving direct expression to belief, as well as various practices integral to such acts, including the building of places of worship, the use of ritual formulae and objects, the display of symbols, and the observance of holidays and days of rest.'[9]

This connection is further affirmed by Human Rights Council Resolution 6/37: 'The Human Rights Council urges States

---

[7] Natan Lerner, *Group Rights and Discrimination in International Law* (2d ed.) (The Hague, London and New York: Martinus Nijhoff Publishers, 2002), 118.

[8] UN Doc. A/RES/55/254 (2001).

[9] UN Human Rights Committee, CCPR General Comment No. 22: Article 18 (Freedom of Thought, Conscience, or Religion), 30 July 1993, CCPR/C/21/Rev.1/Add.4, paragraph 4 (General Comment 22) (emphasis added).

'[t]o exert the utmost efforts, in accordance with their national legislation and in conformity with international human rights and humanitarian law, to ensure that religious places, sites, shrines and symbols are fully respected and protected and to take additional measures in cases where they are vulnerable to desecration or destruction. ... The Human Rights Council urges States [t]o ensure, in particular, the right of all persons to worship or assemble in connection with a religion or belief and to establish and maintain places for these purposes.'[10]

As noted by a leading elaborator of this right, 'The right to establish and maintain places of worship has since been unambiguously entrenched as a constituent element of the right to freedom or belief...'[11]

This right has received further concretization in the broader process of international human rights standard-setting.[12] Over time, this has yielded a detailed set of interpretations of the right to establish and maintain places of worship, which include the following points[13]:

---

[10] Human Rights Council, Resolution 6/37, paras. 9(e) and 9(g) (14 December 2007), available at http://ap.ohchr.org/documents/E/HRC/resolutions/A_HRC_RES_6_37.pdf (accessed 23 July 2020).

[11] Noel G. Villaroman, 'The Right to Establish and Maintain Places of Worship: The Developments of its Normative Content under International Human Rights Law', in Silvio Ferrari and Sabrina Pastorelli, eds., Religion in Public Spaces: A European Perspective (London and New York: Routledge Taylor and Francis Group, 2016), 295, 297.

[12] See, e.g., UN General Assembly Resolution, Setting International Standards in the Field of Human Rights, A/RES/41/120, 4 December 1986; M. Mutua, 'Standard Setting in Human Rights: Critique and Prognosis', Human Rights Quarterly (2007) 29:3, 547-630. For a thorough treatment of the right to places of worship, see Heiner Bielefeldt, Nazila Ghanea, and Michael Wiener, Freedom of Religion or Belief: An International Law Commentary (Oxford University Press, 2016), § 1.3.2, 117-143.

[13] These elements are set forth in Villaroman, supra note 11, at 301.

- The right to acquire ownership or lawful possession of real property for the purpose of building a place of worship,
- The right to build a place of worship and to make necessary repairs, subject only to reasonable local planning regulations,
- The right to solicit and receive voluntary financial and other contributions for the purpose of building a place of worship,
- The right to the unhampered use and enjoyment of a place of worship,
- The right of protection to places of worship against interference by the state and non-state actors,
- The right against discrimination in applications to build a place of worship.

The foregoing points have emerged as vital clarifying aspects of the right to establish and maintain places of worship.[14] Suffice to say that the various points mentioned here are supported by views of the UN Human Rights Committee, by assessments of the UN Human Rights Commission and Council, by reports of successive UN Special Rapporteurs for Freedom of Religion or Belief, and by other developments within the UN system. Moreover, they are supported by the ordinary meaning and the sheer logic of what is significant and important if the right to freedom of religion or belief under the UDHR, the ICCPR, and the 1981 Declaration is to be meaningful and effective.

The right to establish and maintain places of worship, as thus elaborated, is further vindicated by interpretations of the right to freedom of religion or belief provided by regional human rights bodies. Several of the elements of this right presuppose in critical ways the right to acquire legal entity status. Thus, the first element noted above, the right to ac-

---

[14] The support for the various elements of the right to establish and maintain places of worship is described in detail in Villaroman, supra note 11, at 301-320. It is also evident in Bielefeldt, Ghanea, and Wiener, supra note 12, § 1.3.2, 117-143.

quire ownership or lawful possession of real property for the purpose of building a place of worship, presupposes having a legal entity capable of owning property.[15] Similarly, in many jurisdictions, it is impossible to apply for zoning, building permits, or other land use approvals without legal entity status.[16] In fact, acquisition of legal entity status is critical in one way or another to virtually all of the more detailed elements of the right to establish and maintain places of worship mentioned above. This right has long been settled in the United States[17] and has become firmly entrenched in recent years in the decisions of the European Court of Human Rights.[18]

---

[15] Villaroman, supra note 11, at 301-303.

[16] See W. Cole Durham, Jr., 'Facilitating Freedom of Religion or Belief through Religious Association Laws', in Tore Lindholm, W. Cole Durham, Jr., and Bahia G. Tahzib-Lie (eds.), Facilitating Freedom of Religion or Belief: A Deskbook (Koninklijke Brill NV, 2004), 321, 322-25. For an overview of the types of legal entities available in different legal systems, see W. Cole Durham, Jr., 'Legal Status of Religious Organisations: A Comparative Overview', The Review of Faith & International Affairs (2010) 8: 2, 3–14, available at http://www.tandfonline.com/doi/abs/10.1080/15570274.2010.487986?journalCode=rfia20&quickLinkVolume=8&quickLinkIssue=2&quickLinkPage=3&selectedTab=citation&volume=8 (accessed 23 July 2020).

[17] There is no significant case law on this issue in the United States since access to legal entity status for religious organisations has been easily available through non-profit corporations or other vehicles for over a century. See Durham, 'Legal Status of Religious Organisations', supra note 16, at 3-5.

[18] Canea Catholic Church v. Greece, 27 EHRR 521 (1999) (ECtHR, App. No. 25528/94, 16 December 1997) (legal personality of the Roman Catholic Church protected); United Communist Party of Turkey v. Turkey (ECtHR, App. No. 19392/92, January 30, 1998); Sidiropoulos & Others v. Greece (ECtHR, App. No. 26695/95, July 10, 1998); Freedom and Democracy Party (ÖZDEP) v. Turkey (ECtHR, App. No. 23885/94, December 8, 1999); Hasan and Chaush v. Bulgaria (ECtHR, App. No. 30985/96, October 26, 2000); Metropolitan Church of Bessarabia v. Moldova (ECtHR, App. No. 45701/99, December 13, 2001); Moscow Branch of the Salvation Army v. Russia, (ECtHR, App. No. 72881/01,

Further support for various aspects of the right to establish and maintain places of worship is evident from work of the Office of Democratic Institutions and Human Rights (ODIHR) and of the Organisation for Security and Cooperation in Europe (OSCE). In 2014, in Cooperation with the Venice Commission of the Council of Europe, ODIHR published its *Guidelines on the Legal Personality of Religious or Belief Communities* (the 2014 Guidelines).[19] These guidelines are the culmination of nearly thirty-five years of development within the Helsinki process.[20] They are based on experience garnered in many of the world's leading democracies, and also on experience in countries peopled by all of the world's major religions. They represent an up-to-date distillation of the existing international human rights norms and the best thinking and practices regarding the rights of religious and belief communities to acquire legal entity status. They describe the applicable norms from international human rights law, and draw together the expertise and experience of the ODIHR's Advisory Council on Freedom of Religion or Belief, the rich legal expertise of the Venice Commission, and input from numerous experts and NGOs from all corners of the OSCE. They also benefited

---

October 5, 2006); Church of Scientology Moscow v. Russia (ECtHR, App. No. 18147/02, April 5, 2007); Svyato-Mykhaylivska Parafiya v. Ukraine (ECtHR, App. No. 77703/01, September 14, 2007); Kimlya v. Russia (ECtHR, App. Nos. 76836/01, 32782/03, 1 October 2009); Magyar Keresteny Mennonita Egyhaz and Others v. Hungary, ECtHR, App. No. 70945/11 and 8 others (8 April 2014). Full text of all cited decisions of the European Court of Human Rights is available at https://www.strasbourgconsortium.org/portal.case.php?pageId=10 (accessed July 23, 2020).).

[19] OSCE Office for Democratic Institutions and Human Rights, Guidelines on the Legal Personality of Religious or Belief Communities (Warsaw, 2014), available at http://www.osce.org/odihr/139046 (accessed 23 July 2020).

[20] The Helsinki process, now institutionalized as the Organisation for Security and Cooperation in Europe, which comprises the countries of Western Europe, the former Soviet bloc, the United States and Canada (a total of 57 countries from 'Vancouver to Vladivostok moving east').

greatly from developments in the United Nations, its human rights institutions, and the work of successive UN Special Rapporteurs on Freedom of Religion or Belief. The guidelines again confirm the right to acquire legal entity status - the necessary foundation for the right to establish and maintain places of worship. They also set the pattern for non-discriminatory treatment in public processes regarding religious communities. They provide, for example, that such procedures should be 'quick, transparent, fair, inclusive and non-discriminatory'.[21] While the 2014 Guidelines ultimately focus on the right of religion and belief communities to acquire legal personality, they are grounded on a thorough explication of the right to freedom of religion or belief set forth in the opening pages of the document. In that sense, they help lay the foundation for better implementation of FoRB in countless other practical settings.

The 2014 Guidelines reaffirm the continuing validity of an earlier and broader set of guidelines promulgated in 2004,[22] which give soft law validity to several of the other detailed elements of the right to establish and maintain places of worship. The 2004 Guidelines affirm the right of religious organisations to solicit funds,[23] to fair and neutral treatment, to equality and non-discrimination,[24] to neutral treatment in land use[25] and

---

[21] Id., para. 24.

[22] Guidelines for Review of Legislation Pertaining to Religion or Belief, prepared by the OSCE/ODIHR Advisory Panel of Experts on Freedom of Religion or Belief in Consultation with the European Commission for Democracy Through Law (Venice Commission), adopted by the Venice Commission (Venice, 18-19 June 2004), welcomed by the OSCE Parliamentary Assembly (Edinburgh, 5-9 July 2004), available at http://www.osce.org/ odihr/13993 (English) and http://www.osce.org/node/13994 (Russian) (accessed 23 July 2020).

[23] Id. at Section J.1, p. 20.

[24] Id. at Section II.B.3, p. 10.

[25] Id. at Section III.C and III.I, pp. 25, 28.

historical preservation matters[26] and in property disputes involving religious property,[27] and in general to non-arbitrary and non-discriminatory treatment of religious communities.

Recurring Problems in the Protection of Places of Worship

Despite the clarity of the right to establish and maintain places of worship under international law, cases of violation of this right abound. In recent years, accounts of numerous types of interference with this right are all too common: from bulldozing places of worship to refusing to allow them to be built in the first place. Discrimination against unpopular religious groups is a recurring problem at the local level practically everywhere. Countless such problems fill the pages of institutional reports on religious freedom compliance,[28] scholarly commentary on the relevant issues,[29] and the case law of international courts.[30] Instead of attempting a comprehensive review of such cases from around the world, this article provides a more in-depth account of representative cases from Russia.

---

[26] Id.

[27] Id. at III.D., p. 25

[28] See, e.g., annual reports of the United States Department of State, https://www.state.gov/j/drl/rls/irf/, and the United States Commission on International Religious Freedom, https://www.uscirf.gov/reports-briefs/annual-report. Reports of similar bodies in other countries are becoming more common. See, e.g., Annual Report of the European Parliament Intergroup for Religious Freedom and Tolerance, http://www.religiousfreedom.eu/wp-content/uploads/2018/09/RS_report_v6_digital.pdf and its Annex, http://www.religiousfreedom.eu/wp-content/uploads/2018/09/RS_Annex_v1_forprint_withbleed.pdf (accessed 23 July 2020).

[29] See, e.g., Villaroman, supra note 11; Bielefeldt, Ghanea, and Wiener, supra note 12.

[30] Manousssakis v. Greece (ECtHR, App. No. 18748/91,29 August 1996).

As is generally the case with such violations, Russia has accepted broad panoply of international and regional commitments on which expectations with regard to places of worship and numerous other human rights were based. These commitments gave rise to particularly high hopes at the time Russia became a member of the Council of Europe in 1996. Prominent among the commitments made and reaffirmed then were its commitment to implement decisions of the European Court of Human Rights, to bring the law on freedom of religion in line with the European Convention for the Protection of Human Rights and Fundamental Freedoms (ECHR), and to participate in 'political dialogue' with the Council's Committee of Ministers, the body that ultimately seeks to assure compliance with the Convention and the decisions of the European Court of Human Rights implementing the Convention.

Even more significantly, by the mid-1990s, Russia had embraced the processes of *glasnost* and *perestroika*, and had adopted a new constitution committed to the protection of human rights, the rule of law, and widely accepted international norms, including freedom of religion or belief, freedom of expression, and non-discrimination. Among other things, the 1993 Russian Constitution provided for direct application of international norms. Specifically, Article 15.4 provides that

> 'The universally recognised norms of international law and international treaties and agreements of the Russian Federation shall be a component part of its legal system. If an international treaty or agreement of the Russian Federation establishes other rules than those envisaged by law, the rules of the international agreement shall be applied'.[31]

This understanding is even clearer with respect to 'basic rights and liberties'. As declared by Article 17.1, 'The basic rights and liberties in conformity with the commonly recognised principles and norms of the

---

[31] Russian Const., art. 15.4 (emphasis added).

international law *shall be recognised and guaranteed in the Russian Federation and under this Constitution*'.[32]

Thus, the Russian Constitution explicitly establishes that basic rights and liberties, such as freedom of religion, freedom of expression, and non-discrimination, 'shall be recognised and guaranteed'.

A further assurance of Russia's intention to be bound by Council of Europe principles is apparent in Article 46.3 of the Russian Constitution, which assures that Russians can turn to international tribunals, such as the European Court of Human Rights, for vindication of their rights, if national relief is not available. 'In conformity with the international treaties of the Russian Federation, everyone shall have the right to turn to interstate organs concerned with the protection of human rights and liberties when all the means of legal protection available within the state have been exhausted.'[33]

The provision states, as do the rules of the European Court, that individuals must first seek an 'exhaustion of remedies' at home before seeking international relief, but leaves no doubt that Russians should be able to seek and obtain such relief.

Unfortunately, Russia has fulfilled neither the hope expressed at the time of its admission to the Council of Europe nor the promises embodied in its constitution. The Russian government's protection of freedom of religion or belief has not only failed to improve, it has steadily deteriorated. This deterioration has been particularly striking in the case of the Jehovah's Witnesses. In April 2017, Russia's Constitutional Court affirmed a finding that Jehovah's Witnesses are an extremist group,[34] and

---

[32] Russian Const., art 17.1 (emphasis added).

[33] Russian Const., art. 46.3.

[34] Supreme Court of the Russian Federation, Case No. AKPI17-238 (2017) (hereinafter Russia Jehovah's Witness Case). An unofficial English translation by Dmytro Vovk is available at https://www.academia.edu/34294283/ Translation._Russian_Supreme_Court_Decision_on_Ban_on_Jehovahs_Witnesses-Vovk English Translation.pdf (accessed 23 July 2017).

sustained liquidation of the church's legal entity, ordering closure of its headquarters and 395 local chapters, as well as seizure of the organisation's property. After this decision, other religious groups are of course also at risk.[35]

The United States Commission on International Religious Freedom has noted this deterioration in successive annual reports, summarising the situation as follows in its 2017 Report:

> 'Russia represents a unique case among the countries in this report - it is the sole state to have not only continually intensified its repression of religious freedom since USCIRF commenced monitoring it [in 1998], but also to have expanded its repressive policies to the territory of a neighbouring state, by means of military invasion and occupation. Those policies, ranging from administrative harassment to arbitrary imprisonment to extrajudicial killing, are implemented in a fashion that is systematic, ongoing, and egregious.'[36]

In the sphere of sacred sites, the problems arise primarily for critics of the Russian Orthodox Church and for minority religions. With this in mind, it will be helpful to focus on three representative situations in Russia:

- Protecting sacred space from sacrilege,
- Restitution of previously expropriated property, and
- The closing of sacred space.

The first type of situation is represented by the Russian government's handling of the Pussy Riot case. The Pussy Riot rock group

---

[35] See Victoria Arnold, Russia: Jehovah's Witnesses now banned, Forum 18, 18 July 2017, available at https://www.refworld.org/docid/596f0b5f4.html (accessed 23 July 2020).

[36] US Commission on International Religious Freedom, 2017 Report, Russia Chapter.

staged an unauthorised and provocative *guerilla performance* in Moscow's Christ the Redeemer Cathedral, a major landmark in contemporary Moscow built on the site where an earlier church had been destroyed by the communist regime in the 1930s. The Orthodox Church claimed that the performance constituted sacrilege. Russian President, Vladimir Putin, claimed that religious organisations should be protected from such attack performances, because 'the country has very grave memories of the initial period of Soviet rule, when a huge number of priests suffered. Many churches were destroyed, and all our traditional faiths suffered huge damage.' The result was that group leaders were convicted of 'hooliganism motivated by hate speech'. Appeals ultimately found their way to the European Court of Human Rights.[37] The case was obviously rooted in intentionally offensive and polarising behaviour. While one can have some questions about the harshness of the punishment imposed on group members, this is a case when the state did in fact defend sacred space, albeit the space of the prevailing religion.

A second case involves the restitution of St. Isaac's Cathedral, the golden-domed symbol of St. Petersburg. The current building was completed in 1858. The original church built on the site dates to the time of Peter the Great. It was converted into the Museum of the History of Religion and Atheism in the early years of the Soviet Union. Recently, the Mayor of St. Petersburg has agreed to give the building back to the Orthodox Church. Protestors contend that it has become a monument first and a church second. The issues surrounding the return of St. Isaac's resemble those frequently encountered in connection with sacred sites.

---

[37] In its decision in Mariya Alekhina and Others v. Russia (ECtHR, App. No. 38004/12, 17 July 2018), the Court found violations of European Convention prohibitions of inhuman or degrading treatment, and of the performers' right to liberty and security, fair trial, legal assistance, and freedom of expression. The Court accepted that some reaction by the Russian government to the performers' breaching the rules of conduct in a place of worship might have been warranted, but judged that the reaction was exceptionally severe.

The opponents of returning the church contend that it is an example of Orthodox believers receiving preferential treatment. Why, they argue, shouldn't the feelings of non-believers or those in other confessions be respected? For them, the structure has become a symbol of St. Petersburg, and it seems unfair for that symbol to be returned to the Orthodox. Others invoke historical memories, sometimes asserting less than tolerant views. Thus, some criticised those opposed to the transfer in anti-Semitic terms as 'the grandchildren and great-grandchildren of those who destroyed our churches, who jumped out of the Pale of Settlement with revolvers in 1917'. The head of the Hermitage Museum warned that turning the museum back into a church would make Leningrad more provincial.

The Church claimed that its regaining ownership of St. Isaac's would return the cathedral to its original purpose and use as a church, not a museum. The Church also wanted to prove it was capable of making a symbolic statement, thereby solidifying its position as one of the most influential institutions in Russia. Of course, the Church also had a financial interest. St. Isaac's has been one of the most lucrative museums in Russia, with 2.4 million tourists annually. Finally, there were symbolic issues. Patriarch Kiril maintained that the return of the church would be a symbol of reconciliation at the 100 years celebration since the 1917 Revolution. The situation is further complicated by the actual history of the building. St. Isaac's had, in fact, never been owned by the Church. It was too expensive to maintain. It was originally managed by the Imperial Ministry. The St. Isaac's case suggests the complexity of the issues that often arise in restitution cases with buildings that have become significant historical and cultural symbols, as well as places of worship. In this case, returning the site to church control highlights the importance of protecting the religious interest in the site, but other factors cloud the analysis.

In the foregoing two cases, in part because of the influence of the dominant religion, the religious claims prevailed under Russian law. This is in sharp contrast to the treatment received by the Jehovah's Witnesses, where the issue is not protection of sacred space, or returning it to a religious claimant, but the dramatic closing of religious space. Jehovah's Witnesses are known for a variety of religious views, including strong commitment to sharing their religious witness with others, opposition to blood transfusions, and conscientious objection to participating in the military and other types of civic engagement. Significantly, however, they are also known for being peaceful and non-violent. Given that reality, it came as a considerable shock when the Russian Supreme Court affirmed the dissolution of their central religious organisation and its 395 local chapters.[38] In many countries throughout the world, constitutional cases brought by Jehovah's Witnesses have helped shape the constitutional contours of FoRB.[39] Victimizing this group by depriving it of legal entity status on the basis of misguided findings of 'extremism' represents a blatant violation of the right to freedom of religion or belief.

This gets ahead of the story of the series of prosecutions that ultimately culminated in the shutting down of the Jehovah's Witnesses sacred space. A first step was to exploit an overly broad anti-extremism law. The Jehovah's Witnesses' New World Translation of the Holy Scriptures was banned as extremist despite a law prohibiting banning copies or quotations from the Bible as extremist. A local court held that the New World translation of the Bible was not a Bible and thus was not

---

[38] See Russia Jehovah's Witness Case, supra note 34.

[39] For example, leading freedom of religion cases in both the United States and the European Court of Human Rights involved vindication of the rights of Jehovah's Witnesses to engage in missionary activities. Cantwell v. Connecticut, 310 U.S. 296 (1940); Kokkinakis v. Greece (ECtHR, App. No. 14307/88, 25 May 1993).

protected by the law.[40] A variety of other standard publications of the Jehovah's Witnesses have been deemed extremist. Similar treatment has been extended to the works of Islamic theologian Said Nursi, and at one point to the version of the Bhagavad Gita used by the ISKCON (Hare Krishna) movement. Once literature was deemed 'extremist,' it could be confiscated, and dissemination of extremist materials became a criminal offense.

One major factor for identifying Jehovah's Witnesses as extremists is that they make exclusive truth claims. Russian expert witnesses relied on by Russian courts in making 'extremism' findings noted that they claim to be preaching the only true religion, and that all other religions (including Christianity as taught by the Russian Orthodox Church) are false. Of course, many mainline groups are guilty of making such claims. Findings of extremism predicated on these criteria are highly problematic, and certainly not neutral.

Another element in the legal arsenal invoked against the Jehovah's Witnesses is the so-called Yarovaya laws, named after Irina Yarovaya, Chairperson of the State Duma Committee on Security, who spearheaded the passage of the laws in 2016. These laws introduced provisions prohibiting among other things proselytization outside of religious buildings belonging to the missionary's organisation. Engaging in religious teaching in people's homes, for example, was banned. Given Jehovah's Witnesses' commitment to sharing their beliefs, these laws constituted another legal trap.

The Jehovah's Witnesses were not the only group caught in this net. Between June 2016 and July 2017, 193 anti-proselytism cases were

---

[40] See Tom Balmforth, Russia Bans Jehovah's Witnesses' Translation of the Bible, Radio Free Europe, 18 August 2017), https://www.rferl.org/a/russia-jehovahs-witnesses-bible-translation-banned/28684384.html (accessed 23 July 2020).

prosecuted.[41] Of these, fifty-eight were brought against Protestant Evangelicals (excluding Baptists); forty against Jehovah's Witnesses; twenty-six against Baptists; twelve against ISKCON (Hare Krishna); nine against Muslims; three against miscellaneous Jews/Kabbalah groups; three against Seventh-day Adventists; two against unidentified Christians; two against dissident Orthodox believers; and one each against the Salvation Army, the New Apostolic Church, The Church of Jesus Christ of Latter-day Saints, and a Neo-Pagan.[42]

One of the most worrisome concerns is the pattern of prosecutions across Russia that culminated in the dissolution of the Jehovah's Witnesses. It is not clear whether this was a centrally orchestrated pattern of prosecution, or merely an indication of systematic biases in local enforcement agencies across Russia. In either case, the pattern is concerning. The pattern is evident on the face of the Russian Supreme Court decision banning the Jehovah's Witnesses, which is notable for citing the numerous lower court cases that ostensibly justified its opinion without providing any real analysis of the bona fides of those lower court decisions. The use of conclusory references to national prosecution patterns obfuscates the systematic repression which is ongoing.

The pattern consists of a series of seemingly disconnected steps. The first step takes advantage of Russia's vague anti-extremism law to brand various pieces of a group's literature as extremist. The Court noted that ninety-five Jehovah's Witness publications were registered in the Federal Registry of Extremist Materials based on final decisions of lower courts. No detailed description is given about these materials, except to note that they include various normal Jehovah's Witness publications.

---

[41] Victoria Arnold, Russia: One year of "anti-missionary" punishments, Forum 18, 8 August 2017, supra note 35.

[42] Victoria Arnold, Russia: One year of "anti-missionary punishments full listing, Forum 18, 9 August 2017, supra note 35 (paragraph in text summarizes information from extensive list of cases in the full listing of cases in the 9 August article).

There is a generic statement that the documents 'incite religious discord, propagandise exclusivity, and ... promote the superiority and inferiority of citizens based on their religious affiliation'. But there was no analysis examining the arguably questionable grounds for these decisions, and there appeared to be no way to challenge such findings in the ultimate dissolution decision.

The second step was to dissolve various local church units based on continued use and dissemination of these materials (which are of course routinely used elsewhere as a standard part of the religious practices of Jehovah's Witnesses). The third step was to issue a warning to the central body of the Jehovah's Witnesses (or other religions being pursued by similar processes) to cease supporting, participating in, or otherwise contributing to the dissemination of the 'extremist' materials. In the Jehovah's Witness case, this is in fact a warning for the central distribution centre for religious materials to cease fulfilling its basic function of providing needed materials for believers and congregations around the country. Note that the idea of providing a warning is in principle a good administrative step. Normally, it can help a religious group that is operating in good faith and does not realise it is stepping across a legal or administrative line to correct problematic conduct without serious sanction. In the Jehovah's Witness case, however, this administrative process is problematic because it enjoins the religious group from engaging in conduct that is vital to its mission and ought to be protected by religious freedom and freedom of expression norms.

The fourth step follows quickly upon on the running of the warning period that is set in motion by step three. The central organisation can then be accused of failing to take preventative measures aimed at eliminating the reasons for, or the conditions facilitating, extremist activity. The centralised organisation is in effect charged with either complicity or failure to exert adequate controls to bring the local organisations to heel. In effect, the centralised organisation becomes an offender if it fails to support the government in enforcing government policies to which both the centralised organisation and the local congregations object as a matter of conscience. There is of course no effective way to challenge the validity of the underlying state findings of violation, except through a seemingly hopeless battle to contest every local action in courts that appear to be deeply biased against the group's religious beliefs.

The fifth step brings the process to a predictable conclusion. Based on the numerous violations that have been accumulated after the warning, state officials bring an action to liquidate (dissolve) the organisation in question and its affiliates. Key steps in the legal process against Jehovah's Witnesses are proceeding apace. On 20 April 2017, the Russian Supreme Court dissolved the administrative centre of the Jehovah's Witnesses and 395 local religious organisations and banned the practice of the Jehovah's Witness faith. On 17 July 2017, the April decision was upheld by the appellate chamber of the Russian Supreme Court. On 9 October 2017, the Jehovah's Witnesses appealed the Supreme Court decision to the Human Rights Ombudsman, to no apparent effect. On 31 October 2017, the proceeding for distribution of Jehovah Witness property commenced in Krasnoyarsk, a proceeding likely to be replicated at local organisations around the country. A special state commission responsible for full inventory of Jehovah's Witness property has been established.

The result in the Jehovah's Witness case goes to such extreme lengths that it is hard to grasp what is behind it. James Richardson, a noted legal scholar and sociologist, has suggested three possible motivations. First, pressure may be coming from the Russian Orthodox Church, which may be seeking to deter groups that compete for the allegiance of Russian citizens. Second, it is possible that harassment is part of an anti-American campaign that has targeted Jehovah's Witnesses because of their American roots. A third possibility is a typical scapegoat manoeuvre that attempts to distract the populace from Russia's real economic and political problems, both at home and abroad.[43] But in fact, total dissolution seems a radically disproportionate response to any such concerns.

How have the Jehovah's Witnesses responded? Unsurprisingly, they have pursued all possible appeals in Russia. They are also pursuing remedies with the European Court of Human Rights. They have officially stopped their normal religious activities, trying not to provoke the state so as to avoid any further prosecutions of their believers. However, some informal meetings are occurring. It is hard to imagine that groups of friends would totally desist from reading the Bible together. This is nonetheless dangerous. Such meetings are technically illegal, and Orthodox activists have tried to report such events. Arrests of believers, police raids, and searches of private houses confirm that such informal activity is occurring. Human rights organisations and Jehovah's Witness media have reported several cases of discrimination against Jehovah's Witnesses. Other examples of discrimination include job losses for those belonging to the movement.

Some efforts have been made to mount legal defences to the dissolution measures. From January to April 2017, Jehovah's Witnesses transferred seventy-four pieces of real property, worth about 402 million roubles, to Jehovah's Witness entities in Sweden, Austria, Spain, and the United States. The reaction in Russia has been to challenge these moves as feigned transactions. As of June 2017, foreign Jehovah's Witness communities owned 65% of Jehovah's Witness property in Russia: 11.5% was owned by leaders and relatives of Russian branches and 23.5% belonged directly to Russian legal entities. Property owned by private individuals will be harder to confiscate, although a case could

---

[43] James T. Richardson, The battle over Jehovah's Witnesses in Russia, New Eastern European, 25 October 2017, http://neweasterneurope.eu/2017/10/25/battle-jehovahs-witnesses-russia/ (accessed 23 July 2020).

potentially be made that it is property being used for extremist purposes, and then confiscated. While remedies are being pursued in Strasbourg, as noted above, it is hard to say how permanent the damage will have become by the time the case is heard by the ECtHR. Given Russia's desultory compliance with European Court decisions, it is difficult to know how effective remedies pronounced in Strasbourg will turn out to be.

This pattern of shutting down sacred space is highly problematic. It flies in the face of protecting places of worship that the Jehovah's Witnesses have a right to assert, as demonstrated in the second part of this article. A possible saving grace is that the entire process appears to pay at least lip service, and hopefully more, to legal constraints. Every step along the way invokes law and legal determinations. Unfortunately, the laws in question seem to be open to abusive manipulation and discrimination.

To make matters worse, Russia has formalised a process of permitting objections to rulings of the European Court of Human Rights. In July 2015, the Russian Constitutional Court held that Russia could fail to enforce an ECtHR judgment if it is the only possible way to avoid a violation of the fundamental principles and norms of the Russian Constitution.[44] In December 2015, a federal law was passed, which in effect incorporated the July decision into federal law.[45] Based on these developments, in April 2016, the Russian Constitutional Court ruled for the first time that a European Court decision could not be implemented in Russia.[46] This is clearly inconsistent with commitments in the Russian Constitution itself and in commitments that Russia made at the time it

---

[44] Resolution of the Constitutional Court of the Russian Federation No. 21-P of 14 July 2015

[45] Federal Law No.7-FKZ of 14 December 2015.

[46] Anchugov and Gladkov v. Russia (ECtHR, App. nos. 11157/04 and 15162/05, 4 July 2013).

became a member of the Council of Europe,[47] and it bodes ill for enforcement of religious freedom rights of unpopular religious groups.

It remains to see how the entire panoply of remedies from the Council of Europe, including the European Court of Human Rights, will be applied. This should include increasingly effective actions taken by the Council of Europe's Committee of Ministers, which is entrusted with ultimate responsibility for supervising ultimate enforcement of the judgments of the European Court of Human Rights. In addition to its power to pass resolutions, sponsor conferences, and in general, to foster dialogue on ways to enhance human rights compliance, the Council of Ministers has played an increasingly important role in supervising the execution of Strasbourg Court decisions. Given the extent of Russian violations with respect to freedom of religion or belief, it seems surprising that there are not more cases involving Russia's violation of Article 9 of the European Convention that have been subjected to the Council of Minister's 'enhanced supervision' procedures. Certainly, what has happened in the Jehovah's Witness case reveals important structural problems within the Russian system that deserve further attention.

As important as international human rights law is, long experience has shown that such norms are not self-enforcing, and often cannot be imposed by intergovernmental pressure. In many situations, the most effective progress has been made through persistent efforts to hold gov-

---

[47] There are precedents elsewhere for constitutional courts to retain jurisdiction to monitor decisions of an international juridical body to confirm that the international body does not mandate violations of its national constitution. (See, e.g., 'Solange II', Federal Constitutional Court of Germany, judgment no. 73, 339 of 22 October 1986.) But in those cases, there would at least be an obligation to interpret the local constitution in a way that avoids the collision with international decisions to the extent possible. Given Russia's constitutional commitments to freedom of religion, it is difficult to see how the Russian Supreme Court could mount a compelling case that a European Court decision in favor of the Jehovah's Witnesses should not be respected.

ernment officials to principles their states have accepted but have all too easily forgotten. It is important to pursue strategies that encourage dialogue designed to identify and remove practical obstacles to compliance, while reminding officials of the persuasive reasons that justify commitments already made. A particular legal concern is finding ways to prevent the accumulation of a series of seemingly small legal distortions being accumulated to justify major religious repression, as seems to have occurred first in the Jehovah's Witness case. The concern is that the pattern visible in the Jehovah's Witness case may be rolled out to the detriment of other religious groups in coming months. More generally, it is important that the efforts of constitutional and human rights institutions be coordinated so that they reinforce each other, rather than competing for priority of position. Failure to protect the right to establish and maintain places of worship in Russia is an important reminder both of the importance of finding ways to achieve better implementation of this now widely accepted right, and of the significance of protecting freedom of religion or belief values at the core of protecting religious and cultural heritage.

Conclusion

The Russian cases involving Moscow's Christ the Redeemer Cathedral and St. Petersburg's St. Isaac's Cathedral are in many ways more comparable to typical sacred site/cultural heritage cases than the Jehovah's Witness dissolution. Jehovah's Witness Kingdom Halls are unlikely to be selected as UNESCO World Heritage sites, and because of the lower profile of their places of worship, some of the tensions between the general public's interest in a site and the worship interests of individuals at that location disappear. There is no doubt that the outcome in the Jehovah's Witness case is severe. Yet the public interest in restraining extremism that lies behind the outcome of dissolving a religion, and totally shutting it down, is not necessarily different in kind (though it is obviously different in degree) from other public interests that seek to impose limits on worship practices to further historical or cultural concerns that do not take freedom of religion claims sufficiently seriously. In both cases, a major consideration is protecting Russian culture. In any event, the Jehovah's Witness case in Russia is a reminder that even humble sites deserve strong protection.

Looked at from the perspective of standard international religious provisions, the result in the Jehovah's Witness is clearly erroneous. At the very least, it is difficult to see why a less restrictive outcome could not have been found. It is simply not credible to believe that Jehovah's Witnesses pose any serious threat to the stability or public order of Russia. This serves as a general reminder of the importance of searching diligently for less restrictive ways to pursue government policies. More importantly, a government willing to crush a group like the Jehovah's Witnesses is all too likely to search out other scapegoats, or to sacrifice other groups, once the first group is effectively removed from the scene. In the end, if the sacristy of sacred sites, even humble sites, is not protected, the structures that remain will be at best hollow (if not whited) sepulchres.

PART IV

CASE STUDIES
ON CURRENT CHALLENGES

10

AUSTRIA

Dr Peter Krömer, Evangelical Church of the Augsburg Confession in Austria

In general, Austrian law distinguishes three types of legal personalities in relation to the foundation and consecutive recognition of religious communities under the law.

(Privileged) public bodies:

- Pursuant to article 15 of State Constitutional Law of 1876, *Staatsgrundgesetz* provides for religious communities and churches to enjoy the status of a privileged public body, either on the basis of historical recognition, special laws or regulations based on the recognition law of 1874 (*Anerkennungsgesetz*) or the *Islamgesetz*, Islam law of 2015.
- The requirements to become a public body are more complicated than for the other two legal forms. Therefore, the issue of public bodies will be examined separately further on.

Confessional communities:

- Pursuant to the state law concerning the legal personality of confessional communities.
- The requirement for recognition as a confessional community must have a religious community claiming a minimum of 300 members as registered Austrian residents.

Associations:

- Pursuant to the 2002 law on Associations.
- A religious community in Austria with less than 300 members can register as an association.

A fourth option exists for foreign churches or so-called embassy churches. These are churches which are foreign legal personalities recognised in conjunction with the embassy of the respective state in which those churches are constituted. A famous example would be the Anglican Church, seated in the United Kingdom, and registered in Austria as an embassy church with around 500 members.

Religious communities and churches recognised as public bodies (option 1) enjoy special rights and special obligations under the law. In this manner, they differ greatly from confessional communities or simple associations.

Here is a quick overview on how a religious community can become a public body in the first place.

Firstly, a religious community needs to be comprised of a minimum of two *per mille* of a state's population, which means around 17,000 members. The religious community in question must have been active internationally as an organised group and in teaching for a duration of 200 years or within Austria for a duration of ten years. Religious communities already recognised as confessional communities only need to have been active for duration of five years within Austria.

Secondly, religious communities and churches must differ in their teaching from existing churches and religious communities. Their teaching further has to demonstrate a positive, basic attitude towards the state, in particular towards the democratic principles on which a western state such as Austria is founded, including all its basic rights and freedoms.

The requirement for religious communities to demonstrate full acceptance of fundamental and basic human rights and freedoms is particularly interesting and subject to great public debate in relation to the request for recognition of Islamic communities.

Religious communities and churches that have been recognised as public bodies can further acquire such public recognition for their local parishes and other institutions. Recognition for confessional communities, in comparison, is only possible for their local parishes but not for any of their institutions.

Today, both religious communities and churches recognised as public bodies and confessional communities are subject to some rather limited supervision by the so-called *Kultusamt*, which forms part of the office of the federal chancellor. Given that numerous imams in Austria are being paid or even employed by the state of Turkey and allegedly promote and incite terrorist activities, there is currently a strong public debate and desire for stronger supervision of Islamic religious communities. It is hard to tell what consequences this will bear for other religious communities and churches.

Associations (the third form of legal personality) are generally under much stronger supervision than religious communities and confessional communities, as they are under the supervision of the general administrative bodies, which are ultimately headed by the Minister of Interior Affairs. This ultimate supervision by the minster is quite problematic from the point of view of constitutional law.

Further, it is noteworthy that religious communities and churches recognised as public bodies still only benefit from a portion of these privileges and are still treated in a special manner. This kind of treatment has oftentimes and perhaps rightly, been criticised and even ultimately led to the constitutional court deciding to grant more privileges to religious communities and churches, details of which would go beyond the scope of this presentation.

The European Court of Human Rights has so far never criticised the Austrian system for its three types of legal personality or the supervisory system, which is limited for confessional communities and public bodies and stronger for associations. In fact, it pointed out that the Austrian system complies with the European Convention on Human Rights.

All three types of legal personalities (public bodies, confessional communities and associations), including the fourth type (foreign churches, including their parishes and institutions that have acquired legal personality) can acquire properties according to the general principles of private law, with or without any buildings. In this regard, religious communities and churches, irrespective of their legal form, are treated equally to other public bodies under the law. Thus, internally binding acts do not suffice for a property transaction among different church parishes and have to be handled like any other transaction. The same holds true for rental agreements, which must be concluded in the same manner as any other rental agreement.

The following points are important in Austria in relation to the acquisition of property for any legal person, public and/or private, and oftentimes are unknown to representatives of religious communities and churches.

Each of the nine, small Austrian states possesses its own special laws restricting the acquisition and use of property rights related to land utilised for the purposes of agriculture and forestry (*Grundverkehrsgesetz*). These laws further restrict the acquisition of property by foreigners and for all purchases concerning a second home (for citizens not registered in this city or region). This is to ensure that as few properties as possible are acquired for the purposes of a second home or holiday home. For religious communities and churches, this means that no property can be purchased unless the priest is registered in this specific city.

Furthermore, the acquisition of property, as well as long-term rental agreements is restricted for legal personalities, which are seated outside of the European Union and the European Economic Area and Switzerland.

These kinds of restrictions also naturally apply to religious communities and churches not exempt from the standard rules and thus also to so-called foreign churches or embassy churches mentioned at the beginning. Churches seated outside of the European Union and the European Economic Area and Switzerland may be subject to additional restrictions in relation to the acquisition of property and the renting of (church) buildings.

The competence of regulating regional development, regional planning and construction also falls under the authority of each state. Thus, there are nine different regulations governing these matters. Regional planning includes criteria for determining the designation of property for construction, agriculture or forestry purposes. Construction laws regulate the conditions for all types of constructions, including church buildings, worship rooms and the like. These laws apply to churches and religious communities in the same manner as they do to any other private or public legal person/entity with no exception.

According to regional development laws, church buildings and other places of worship can generally be built on any type of land except for purported grassland. Certain regional planning laws provide special regulations for church buildings and other places of worship, which grant special designation of land to the construction of churches and worship buildings. Some regions grant exceptions to construction requirements with regard to issues of height, for example.

It is noteworthy that no such exceptions exist for the building of confessional communities and religious associations. In Austria, two Islamic communities are recognised as religious communities and are thus privileged public bodies rather than confessional groups. As they could be granted potential exceptions, the state of Carinthia debated the introduction of a general prohibition to the construction of mosques with minarets. Eventually, no such prohibition was introduced.

It should come as no surprise that churches and religious communities of whatever legal form require building permits for the construction of its churches or religious buildings. These permits are also required if changes to existing buildings are planned. There are two specialities when it comes to churches or religious communities:

- Religious communities and churches recognised as public bodies are exempt from the special state provisions related to the construction of functional rooms. These construction provisions constitute special types of provisions.

- Rooms used for worship by religious communities and churches recognised as public bodies are exempt from special employment regulations concerning the protection and security of employees. These laws provide for special construction measures related to the security of employees working within these spaces. These exemptions do not apply to confessional communities and (religious) associations, which oftentimes leads to problems in practice. For example, in the case of Evangelical Free Churches, which are confessional communities in Austria, issues arose in relation to the construction of the baptismal font. When the Free Churches wanted a big font to be built in the middle of the church for the occasional use of baptisms, they were asked by the local authorities to construct permanent railings around the font to comply with the security and protection law for employees, for which there is no exemption for confessional communities (unlike religious communities recognised as public bodies).

Another legal aspect to consider when referring to property, in particular with concern to church buildings and other old buildings, is urban heritage conservation. Generally, it is possible for any historical or culturally important building to be put under special monument protection, irrespective of the owner. In practice, only church buildings, monasteries and other special building of religious communities and churches recognised as public bodies are declared to be under special monument protection regulation or, in other words, part of the urban heritage conservation. This results in financial issues for churches and religious communities, sometimes to great financial burden, since maintenance of these old buildings is expensive, as they have to be preserved in a certain manner. Further, any desired change of the building for a liturgical reason, for example, requires permission from the Federal Monuments office; as such buildings are a protected heritage. Proceedings before the Federal Monuments office can be tricky as, to be accepted, any reason for a desired alteration must be found in the liturgical regulations. Determining which practices actually constitute liturgical regulations is difficult and thus causes the greatest practical problems for churches, especially with regard to older buildings.

Irrespective of the legal status of the religious community or the church, all religious buildings fall under a special, namely more stringent, legal protection against criminal damages.

The good news is that any religious communities and churches, including their parishes, that are recognised as public bodies enjoy privileges with regard to estate taxes (property, including building structure). When an estate of religious communities and churches is recognised as a public body and used for the purposes of pastoral care, religious teaching and, in some instances, elderly care, no property tax has to be paid.

This privilege does not extend to religious associations and confessional communities.

There is another tax exemption related to the acquisition of property. It only has a very limited scope of application, which, in practice, means that very few religious communities and churches recognised as public bodies are exempt from taxes in connection to the acquisition and purchase of property. Again, no exemption applies to religious associations and confessional communities, not even in theory.

Taxes also incur at the sale of property in Austria (with or without a building structure) and there are no exceptions or privileges for religious communities of any kind. This often causes an additional financial burden for parishes.

11

GREECE

Rev. Meletis Meletiadis, Evangelical Church of Greece

The passing of law 4301 by the Greek Parliament in 2014 not only recognised churches that applied for official state recognition and were included in it, but it also solved many of the chronic problems these churches were facing. In a way, the law answered the first concern, which is stated in CEC's Letter of Invitation to this conference[1]. 'The effective and comprehensive protection of Holy Sites through legal tools and public policy are key for the development of social cohesion in inclusive, confident and tolerant societies.'

Since the law passed, the political will of the Ministry of Culture, Education and Religions is evident in initiatives like the creation of the 'Network of recording and evaluating the desecration and vandalism of religious sites' and in its first document published in 2016.

However, the following sentence of the Invitation Letter is lacking in Greece. 'Reversely, restrictions relating to their use... add to social erosion [and] fragmentation...'

Since the implementation of the law, there have been a number of issues to arise that need to be addressed so that the desired goal of the aforementioned law can be effective, namely equal treatment between

---

[1] See annex.

the majority church and the minority churches in the Greek state. To that effect, on 9 March 2016, the Evangelical Church of Greece, along with all the other churches recognised by the law, submitted a letter to the Ministry of Culture, Education and Religions, along with a memorandum of proposed recommendations to the law.

The following recommendations are relevant to the subject of this article.

Places of Worship

The letter proposed that places of worship of all recognised religious and ecclesiastical entities benefit from equal status and be treated the same way in matters pertaining to administration, tax obligations and urban planning regulations, with the corresponding buildings and facilities of the Orthodox Church (temples, chapels, monasteries, places of prayer, etc.).

This is an urgent necessity because, while there are court decisions for this, i.e. those of the Supreme Administrative Court of Greece and the opinions of the Legal Council of State accepted by the Minister of Finance, the various departments apply any interpretation of the law they deem applicable in each situation. Likewise, the various local officials of the same department, i.e. Tax Bureau, etc., apply personal and subjective interpretations.

To give an example, in 1989 the property of the Evangelical Church of Katerini in Leptokarya, which was used as a children's and family camp, was included in the city plan as per a decision carried out in 2005. As a result, the church was obliged to make payments of land and money, thereby reducing the size of the remaining property and its net worth. Lawsuits brought by the Church against the administration for compensation for property and non-pecuniary damages, *ηθική βλάβη*, were dismissed by the first and second degree courts. The Church appealed to the Supreme Administrative Court of Greece. The appeal was heard in April 2018.

One of the reasons for the appeal was the operative use of the property as a place of worship. So far the courts have rejected the claim arguing that religious services (liturgies, sermons, festivals) do not confer the status of sanctuary to the particular property given that no license has been provided by an administrative authority to establish a sanctuary in the camp premises.

However, according to Supreme Administrative Court jurisprudence in a case concerning the Orthodox Church, it was decided that articles 13 (religious freedom) and 24 (environmental protection) of the Constitution should be interpreted in such a way that the religious element be included as part of the cultural environment, protected by article 24. The religious element is a part of the culture of every people, whereas the places of religious activity and worship, as places for the exercise of religious duties for both clergy and faithful, are a religious and cultural element protected by the Constitution and the laws.

Even if the sites are not directly religious in nature (i.e. are not sacred temples), but have the element of sanctity and are used in the exercise of religious freedom by the purpose they serve and by their very nature, the state servants must justify decisions specifically on grounds of public interest, which make restrictions of the right to freedom of religion necessary, especially when there are no other milder means. In the present case, the administration did not provide any justification for intervening in the constitutionally protected property and certainly did not prove that the principle of proportionality was respected before the act was adopted. There is no evidence to prove that the right to freedom of religion will have to retreat to the rights of third parties. In addition, had other milder means been applied in the implementation of the city plan, the character of the property as an area where religious and liturgical activities take place would not have been affected.

After the publication of law 4301/2014, worship places of the Evangelical Church of Greece are designated as holy temples and may have annexes, which are also places of worship. In light of the implementation of the new law, the camp site in Leptokaria serves as an annex to the Church of Katerini parish. Consequently, the Supreme Administrative Court of Greece is expected to judge the correct interpretation of the Constitution and the new legal situation according to its own case law.

Thus, in order to avoid irregularities in services provided by the civil servants and the trying experience of being at the mercy and whim of any civil servant, an addition to article 13 of the Law 4301/2014 was proposed.

Financial Matters

The fact is that from the inception of the Greek state there has not been any form of religious law, which would have dealt with a host of matters. Therefore, all religious bodies (apart from Orthodox, Muslim and Jewish) have used existing civil law to manage their growing properties. Thus, they created private entities (foundations) to act as owners of those properties, for which legal fees and taxes were of course paid every time, as the law demanded.

With the new law, religious and ecclesiastical bodies can now own their own properties and they are, accordingly, working to transfer them from those legal entities to which they had lent them. However, the state is once again asking these religious and ecclesiastical bodies to pay fees and taxes to have their properties transferred.

This would not pose a problem were the amounts nominal but they are calculated in relation to the property's market value, which is related to its locality. This means that in order to take ownership of what is theirs, and for which they have already paid notary fees and state taxes, local churches are being called to pay a second time for the same property and this time in the millions.

Thus, the Greek state is being asked to allow religious and ecclesiastical entities to transfer their properties free of charge and at only 0,01% of its market value in notary fees.

Ecclesiastical and Religious Legal Entities are Religious and Non-profit

No public employee would question the religious and non-profit character of the Orthodox Church and its many organisations and institutions. Yet there is a very serious issue in the way the administration's apparatus deals with the other churches, as they often encounter difficulties in issuing tax numbers and assigning a tax credit to the NACE Classification, *αντιστοίχιση ΚΑΔ*, as well as imposing inheritance tax precisely because the Tax Bureau declares ignorance of the non-profit character of these churches.

Consequently, the Greek state is being asked to ensure that its employees are aware that ecclesiastical and religious legal entities are religious and have a non-profit status.

Ancient Artefacts

Since this article refers to 'Places of Worship and Holy Sites in Europe and the Middle East: Status and Protection under National and International Law', places of worship which are related to Greece's ancestral religion must be included.

In the past, and while Greece was under various occupational forces and could not order the country's fortune, there has been extensive removal of artefacts from ancient temples, tombs and archaeological sites. Today, many of those artefacts adorn displays in museums of northern Europe and the British Isles.

Protestant Greeks would ask that readers of this article advocate and support Greece's drive to repatriate every artefact that was taken away from Greek territory and that they are returned to their original and natural place. It is a matter of justice and cultural justice. The remaining marbles of the Acropolis of Athens, today placed in the New Acropolis Museum, are a reminder and a call for cultural justice to be served.

12

UKRAINE

Dr Antoine Arjakovsky, Collège des Bernardins, France

This proposition may be criticized or quickly classified as utopian or even dangerous, as has happened in the past to many original ideas which were realised all the same. This is a proposition of peace and may those who criticise it propose better ideas that will truly aid in putting an end to the actual crisis of Orthodox ecclesial governance.

The Russian-Ukrainian Conflict of Ecclesial Jurisdictions

The two laws being discussed at the Rada of Kiev since 2016 concern a new procedure of accreditation of religious leaders in Ukraine who depend on a Church situated in an antagonist country (n. 4511) and the modalities of the changing jurisdictions for religious communities (n. 4128). The patriarchate of Moscow considers that these laws discriminate against the Ukrainian Orthodox Church which depends on its jurisdiction. It insists that the properties of religious communities depend on the archbishop's decision and that the members of these religious communities cannot be those who answer the question on an eventual change of jurisdiction.

Using statistics to defend their argument, in May 2017, the Ukrainian authorities replied that, firstly, they do not discriminate against any church when it sends documents requesting their communities be registered if the documents have been filled out in good and due form.[1] Secondly, they affirm that, according to the law in force in Ukraine, the churches do not have juridical personality, which is why only religious entities (parishes, monasteries etc...) can make decisions and own property. Ukrainian law, in conformity with the European Court of Human Rights, has always defended this principle.

Law n. 4128, supported in particular by the Ukrainian government but also by well-known orthodox personalities such as the deacon of the Russian Church, Andrei Kurayev, and the Ukrainian Archimandrite, Cyrille Hovorun, specifies that members of a community are those who protect the parish from decisions that could be made by transitory tourists.[2] The Ukrainian authorities go on to explain that likewise, in accordance with law 4511 and with the consent of the OSCE (Organisation of Security and Cooperation in Europe) and given the state of war with Russia, they want to have the means to stop the activities of ecclesiastical leaders who could be found to have links with terrorist organisations. Moreover, the Ukrainian authorities reproach the Russian Duma for having adopted, in June 2016, new laws that went against liberty of conscience and which impeded the missionary work of the churches without any protestation on the part of Patriarch Kirill.[3]

Taking into account the virulent reactions of the patriarchate of Moscow, as well as of Roman Catholic Church representatives, which were afraid of losing a good part of their places of worship if the faithful had a voice equivalent to their hierarchical authorities and, finally, of the

---

[1]   https://www.obozrevatel.com/ukr/society/68410-zalucheni-chimali-koshti-v-radi -rozpovili-yak-kremlvikoristovue-upts-mp.htm

[2] https://risu.org.ua/ua/index/exclusive/review/67079/

[3] https://risu.org.ua/ua/index/expert_thought/open_theme/68165

risk of seeing the Ukrainian state enter into the churches' decision-making process (N.B. the Patriarch of Moscow has not been authorised to enter the Ukraine since the beginning of the Russian-Ukrainian war), these laws have not been submitted to the vote of the deputies.

For his part, Bishop Evstrati Zoria, spokesperson of the Ukrainian Orthodox Church (patriarchate of Kiev) proposed some compromises.[4] He suggests, on the one hand, a third legal project which asks for precise clarification to define the membership of parishes to their original juris-diction with the project of law 4511. He requests that it be specified that the state not be able to name an ecclesiastical personality but only exer-cise the right to accept or refuse the nomination of a bishop (just as the Pope has the right to refuse the nomination of an ambassador). In addi-tion, the patriarchate of Kiev is proposing to other churches that parish-ioners' request to change jurisdiction be dependent on a certain number before becoming valid (e.g. two-thirds) and that the minority parishion-ers enjoy the alternative possibility of celebrating elsewhere or in the same building.

These two laws will probably be rewritten and submitted to the vote of the deputies during the months to come. On 7 September 2017, Presi-dent Porochenko notified the Rada that he would not sign law 4511 in its actual form. He already disposes of all the legal means for preventing hybrid attempts, already unfortunately identified by several observers of collusion between certain representatives of the patriarchate of Moscow and the Russian terrorist forces installed in Donetsk, notably the Ortho-dox Army of Donbas[5] which is led by a Russian, Mikhail Verin.[6]

---

[4] https://risu.org.ua/ua/index/monitoring/society_digest/67131/

[5] https://stopterror.in.ua/info/2015/11/russkaya-pravoslavnaya-ameriya-tak-nazy vaemoj-donetskoj-narodnojrespubliki/

[6] https://www.svoboda.org/a/28746740.html

The Persistent Conflict between the Churches of Moscow and Constantinople and a Possible Solution

The real conflict, however, is being played out between the patriarchate of Moscow and the patriarchate of Constantinople, not only concerning the status and control of the Ukrainian Orthodox Church but, above all, concerning the control of the Orthodox Church as a whole. It is a well-known fact that the Church of Kiev historically sees the Moscow Church as a daughter and not as a mother. On the other hand, the patriarchate of Moscow considers itself the unique heir of the Church of Kiev and has tried to impose its dominion over Ukrainian Orthodoxy ever since the latter chose to recognise the Council of Florence in 1439.

Much has been written about the fact that, should the Church of Moscow lose its jurisdiction over Ukraine, not only would it lose a great number of parishes and ecclesiastical structures but, above all, it would mean the end of its grandiose project of becoming the Third Rome, the beacon not only of Orthodoxy but of the whole Church of Christ. Conscious of the decisive importance of this religious factor in the Russian-Ukrainian project, in September 2017 President Petro Porochenko, himself an Orthodox, pronounced himself in favour of recognition of the autocephaly of the Ukrainian Orthodox Church by Constantinople.[7]

In the month of September 2017, the Ukrainian deputy Victor Yelensky pointed out that the Patriarch of Constantinople had not replied to the June 2016 request of the Rada nor to that of President Porochenko to recognise the autocephaly of the Orthodox Church of Kiev for fear that the Church of Moscow would lose the majority of its communities and react by severing all ties with Constantinople.[8]

To get out of the conflict and, above all, to avoid provoking other wars, it would be useful to study the feasibility of the Ecumenical Patri-

---

[7] https://risu.org.ua/ua/index/all_news/state/national_religious_question/68183
[8] https://risu.org.ua/ua/index/all_news/community/religion_and_policy/68205

archate opening a Pan-Orthodox office in Kiev. This would not only facilitate reconciliation among Christians in Ukraine but would also be more perfectly faithful to its mission of pan-Orthodox supervision which it inherited after the rupture between the eastern Christian world and the western Christian world after the fall of Constantinople in 1453. It could then offer an autocephalic organisation to the more than 1000-year-old local Ukrainian Church, and allow it to elect its own primate while positioning itself in a privileged space for presiding over and administering to the communion of Orthodox churches. It would put into practice the principle of inter-jurisdictional episcopal assemblies on the territory of the mother churches, which already function in the countries of what is known as the *diaspora*, i.e. three-quarters of the planet, and which was formally adopted at the Council of Kolymbari in June 2016.

Originally, the concept of the episcopal see was not static. It moved around in function of historical circumstances. It would be useful to recover its original dynamic connotation. Its meaning was not to give a satisfied repose from history but to *receive the divine wisdom.*

The famous French constitutionalist Maurice Hauriou wrote that 'the law is a kind of conduct which aims at achieving order in justice'[9]. This is why an institution like the patriarchate of Constantinople, whose mission since the rejection of the Council of Florence is to permit communion among those who confess the Orthodox faith, should position itself above juridical normativism and in the name of the common good.

---

[9] Maurice Hauriou, « L'ordre social, la justice et le droit », in: Revue trimestrielle de droit civil, 1927, p. 820 (reprint to be found in: Aux sources du droit. Le pouvoir, l'ordre et la liberté. Cahiers de la Nouvelle Journée, Paris, 1933, 23, p. 43-71.

The Arguments in Favour of a Pan-Orthodox Representation of the See of Constantinople at Kiev

Following the baptism of Vladimir the Prince of Kiev in 988, *de jure,* the Rus' of Kiev, found itself in the patriarchate of Constantinople's ecclesial jurisdiction. The Patriarch of Constantinople sent bishops there until the 15th century and his authority was recognised by the Metropolitan of Kiev, Petro Mohyla, until the 17th century. Constantinople never recognised the Russian Church synod's annexation of the metropolis of Kiev (1686) after the invasion of the lands situated on the right bank of the Dnieper River by the Russian Empire. Moreover, as of 1721, the Church of Moscow, whose status of autocephaly had been snatched from Constantinople in 1588, lost its status as a patriarchate by a decree from Peter the Great. This was brought up again in Kiev in August 2016 by Bishop Job of Telmessos, the envoy of Patriarch Bartholomeus to Ukraine. Additionally, the Ukrainian Orthodox Church of Immigrants to the United States and Canada was spontaneously placed under the jurisdiction of Constantinople following the fall of the Berlin Wall.

By opening a pan-Orthodox representation in Kiev, the Patriarch of Constantinople would be able to place all the Orthodox bishops under the authority of an assembly of bishops, something Moscow had been incapable of creating after the 1991 schism between the Ukrainian Orthodox Churches of the patriarchate of Kiev and those of the patriarchate of Moscow. Those who refused would then fall under the direct jurisdiction of Moscow but they would henceforth be obliged to satisfy the conditions of Ukrainian State control imposed on churches situated in antagonistic countries. The head of this Church would initially have autonomy and then accede to autocephaly on the occasion of a new patriarchal election open to the various jurisdictions present in Ukraine.

In so doing, the Ecumenical Patriarch would be extensively criticized by the Russian Patriarch. This act could lead to a rupture of communion between the two Sees of Moscow and Constantinople, as it did in 1996 after the re-establishment of the Estonian Orthodox Church, directed by a Greek Metropolitan. On the one hand, Patriarch Kirill did not recognise the authority of Patriarch Bartholomeus when he refused to attend the June 2016 pan-Orthodox Council in Crete, a move which already placed him in a situation of schism, at least on the level of ecclesial governance. On the other hand, Patriarch Kirill has not hesitated to create para-ecclesial structures in the Near East and in Turkey on canonical territory directly under the Patriarch of Constantinople. In 2017, Sergei Stepachin, the Russian general of the FSB (Federal Security Service), simply informed the Patriarch of Constantinople of the creation of an antenna of the Imperial Orthodox Society of Palestine in Turkey.[10] This latter recuperates or redeems places of worship on Byzantine patriarchate canonical territory. In France, the Orthodox Cathedral of Nice was removed from the patriarchate of Constantinople's jurisdiction by the Russian state courts with the support of the patriarchate of Moscow. The Patriarch of Constantinople does not have much to lose since his authority is continually and publicly questioned by the Patriarch of Moscow.[11]

The advantage the Ecumenical Patriarchate would gain from such a gesture is three-fold. For one, it would regulate 90% of the problem of Orthodoxy divisions within the second largest Orthodox nation in the world. Many already know that three-quarters of 25 million Ukrainian Orthodox Christians are presently under the patriarchate of Kiev's jurisdiction.[12] Moreover, it is estimated that more than three quarters of the

---

[10] http://www.dsnews.ua/society/vzyat-konstantinopol-kak-fsb-skupaet-pravosla vnye-svyatyni-171020000

[11] https://mospat.ru/en/2013/12/26/news96344/

[12] In 2016 as a whole, 38.4% of the Ukrainians declared themselves members of the Orthodox patriarchate of Kiev whereas 17.4% declared that they belonged to the patriarchate of Moscow. But due to the fact of the so9viet history of the Ukraine, there are twice as many parishes registered as belonging to the patriar-

remaining faithful - 25% from the patriarchate of Moscow and the autocephalous Church - would join this new assembly of bishops, as demonstrated since 2014 by the transfer of parishes from the patriarchate of Moscow to the patriarchate of Kiev.

Secondly, it would enable the assembly of bishops to find state protection on executive and legislative levels, and procure financial assistance and, above all, benefit from more breathing room than the Turkish government allows. Indeed, this government blocks all missionary activity, even to the point of refusing the return of the patriarchate's school of theology on the island of Halki. In addition, the Orthodox live with the myth that only the imperial city fell in 1453, and not the ecclesial See of Constantinople, in spite of the painful evidence of the closing of the Cathedral of Saint Sophia, the end of the Church's political privileges and the progressive shrinking of its ecclesial role in the Phanar. This rejection of reality is, above all, a sign of the incapacity of Orthodox Christians to accept the role of history and human freedom in the mystery of the divine-humanity.

By having contact with the Ukrainian Church, the patriarch would also be able to advance his reformation project within Orthodoxy. Imagine for a moment that the churches of the Greek tradition had not always attained the level of consciousness of the 1917 Council of the Russian Church, as they have not always recognised the decisions and orientations of this Council (elections of the bishops, ecumenical involvement, the translation of liturgical texts, the social commitment of the laity, etc.). This would have led to an absurd situation where the bishops elected according to the rulings of the Council of Moscow and under the jurisdiction of Constantinople (the Russian parishes of the exarchate of France and those within the Orthodox Church in the United States) would not be recognised by the patriarchate of Constantinople.

---

chate of Moscow (about 10,000) than to the patriarchate of Kiev. https://risu.org.ua/ua/ondex/expert_thought/open_theme/67281/

Conclusion

Prophetic gestures are often productive in the long-term. In the West, Roman popes only became powerful after they went to Avignon. Olivier Clement imagined an itinerant See for the Patriarch of Constantinople beginning with the island of Patmos. When Patriarch Athenagoras presided at the Center of Chambesy opening, he had the same vision of organising its federative mission of preparation for the pan-Orthodox Council and ecumenical witness before international institutions (United Nations, World Council of Churches) with Switzerland as its base. But the historical advantage of the Ukrainian Church over Greece and Switzerland is that this Church is its direct daughter, the living fruit of its missionary activity and a place of future reconciliation with the Church of Moscow.

Paradoxically, by leaving Istanbul and immersing itself in history, by facilitating the reopening of worship in the Cathedral of Hagia Sophia of Kiev (certainly with the support of the Greek Catholic Ukrainian Church, which has never ceased to affirm its adherence to the Byzantine tradition), the patriarchate of Istanbul, which was not able to prevent the sultans' closing of Hagia Sophia of Constantinople, would be able to actualize its role as primate of the whole Orthodox world. By recovering its liberty of action, it could also advance more firmly in its fraternal relationships with the Protestant and Catholic Churches.

Finally, by putting into place a post-ethnic governance of the Church, as was proposed by the Fathers of the Council of Kolymbari, it would open the way to the progressive end of the political-ethnic-religious conflict between Russia and Ukraine, as well as to the disputes which tear apart other local churches. After all, the geo-political dream of Orthodoxy can no longer be the Empire of Constantinople nor the eternal status of *dhimmi* (the status of non-Muslims in a Muslim state), even less a post-modern or neo-Russian version of Byzantine symphony - that unfortunate invention of Eusebius.

The geo-political vision of the Orthodox Church can only be that of an encounter with the Divine Wisdom, which is nothing other than the vision of Saint John the Evangelist in his Book of Revelation.

13

ROMANIA

Fr. Dr Sorin Selaru, Romanian Orthodox Church

Introduction

In Romania, there currently are 18 legally recognised cults (religions)[1] Concerning these, the Romanian Constitution provides that 'religious cults shall be autonomous from the State and shall enjoy support from it…' (Art. 29, 5). Law no. 489/2006 on Freedom of Religion and the General Status of the Cults in Romania foresees that, as a rule, the expenses involved by maintaining the churches and religious communities and carrying out their activities are to be covered by their own means, obtained and used in accordance with their statutes. The financial assistance provided, upon request, by the state is fixed depending on the number of members of a religious community (principle of proportionality), as well as on its real operational needs. As a rule, this amount can be used to cover operational costs, the construction or maintenance of real estate, or financing social, cultural and educational programs.[2]

---

[1] Besides these, there also are 30 other registered religious associations.

[2] See the study of the Representation of the Romanian Patriarchate to the EU, The Financing of the Churches and Religious Communities in the EU, Bucharest: Basilica, 2014.

The central state authority in charge of this field is the government's State Secretariat for Religious Affairs (Cults), whose status is defined by each new government, upon its investiture. The State Secretariat also administers budget funds earmarked for the construction and restoration of houses of worship and for the restoration of churches considered historic monuments (about 30-35% of its annual budget). The local authorities may also finance, by county/local council ordinance, the construction or restoration of houses of worship and various other projects initiated by religious organisations.

A recent statistical analysis by the Romanian State Secretariat for Religious Affairs on the number of places of worship in Romania, revealed that, at the beginning of 2015, the Orthodox faithful, representing 86.45% of the Romanian population according to the latest census (2011), own 59.9% of the total number of 27,384 places of worship (i.e. there currently are 16,403 Orthodox places of worship throughout the country), while the other officially recognised religious denominations own 40.1%.[3]

In a broader perspective, from amongst the topics related to places of worship currently topping the agenda of Romanian mass-media, the following should be mentioned:

- The project to build a mega-mosque in the centre of Bucharest, with money coming from the Turkish Government. In May 2015, the Romanian Government approved the transfer of 11,000 m^2 to the Muslim Cult of Romania free of charge for the building of this mosque.
- The financial support offered by the State for the construction of the National Orthodox Cathedral in Bucharest (as foreseen by the Emergency Government Ordinance no. 19/2005 regarding the construction of the Architectural Complex of the National Cathe-

---

[3] See http://culte.gov.ro/?page_id=130

dral and law no. 376/2007 for the amendment of para. (2) of art. 1 of Emergency Government Ordinance no. 19/2005 regarding the construction of the Architectural Complex of the National Cathedral).

- The very delicate issue of the patrimonial dispute between the Greek-Catholic (Uniate) and the Orthodox Church, concerning the legal status of ecclesial properties (churches, parish houses and cemeteries).

Dispossession and Change of Owner

The final above point opens the topic on the dispossession and change of owner. What follows is an outline of the case of a church that was transferred to the ownership of the Romanian Orthodox Church during the communist regime. Having been called to judge this case, the Great Chamber of the European Court of Human Rights published its decision in the case Greek-Catholic Parish of Lupeni and Others v. Romania in November 2016.

Historical Background

In December 1948, the communist regime outlawed the Greek-Catholic Church in Romania by Government Decree no. 358. This dramatic moment was preceded by the transfer of over 430 Greek-Catholic priests, together with their communities, to the canonical rule of the Romanian Orthodox Church. All the properties of the Greek-Catholic Church, other than ecclesial, were transferred to the state. An inter-ministerial commission, formed by representatives of the Ministries of Cults, Finances, Internal Affairs, Agriculture, Public Domains and Education, was charged with the task of deciding the fate of these ecclesial properties. The final decision (Decree no. 177/1948) was that they would be transferred to the Orthodox communities.

After the fall of the communist regime in Romania, the Legislative Decree no. 9/31 December 1989 abrogated the Decree no. 358/1948. The Greek-Catholic Church was legally recognised a few months later through the Legislative Decree no. 126/1990 on some measures concerning the Romanian Church united to Rome (Greek Catholic). Article 3 of this Decree provided that the legal status of churches and parish houses, which belonged to the Greek Catholic Church and were transferred to the Orthodox Church, would be settled by a mixed commission formed by representatives of the two cults. In reaching this goal, the commission was supposed to take into consideration the desires of the faithful in the communities that owned these properties. The main issue was that the great majority of the former Greek Catholic faithful and their descendants chose to remain Orthodox, even after the re-establishment of the Greek Catholic Church in Romania in 1990. While the Greek Catholic Church represented almost 8% of the population of the country before 1948, today this figure is below 1%. They currently own 413 places of worship (1.5% of the total number country-wide).

The same Decree in art. 4 foresaw that 'in the municipalities where the number of places of worship is insufficient in relation to the number of worshippers, the state shall provide support for the construction of new churches; for that purpose, it shall make available to the denominations concerned the necessary land if they do not have it, and shall contribute to raising the necessary funds'.

The mixed commission held meetings until 2003 when it was decided that, given the complexity of the various situations, it would be more expedient for the dialogue to continue at the local level for each property.

Confronted by this litigation context, the state amended art. 3 of Legislative Decree no. 126/1990 by Government Ordinance no. 64/2004 and by law no. 182/2005. According to these new amendments, whenever the two communities cannot reach an agreement within the mixed commission, the interested party has the possibility of bringing the case to a civil court, according to common law.[4]

In the explanatory memorandum on this law, it is stated that 'the present law explicitly invests the courts with jurisdiction to rule on the disputes which concern properties which belonged to the Romanian Church united to Rome, where the committees provided for in art. 3 of Legislative Decree no. 126/1990 do not reach an agreement. In order to enable both parties to take measures to resolve the problem of the places of worship in issue, the order allows for continued activity by the committees, offering the possibility of resolving the question of restitution of these premises through inter-denominational dialogue'.

At this point, it should be emphasised that the Romanian Constitutional Court has twice received a plea of unconstitutionality with regard to art. 3 §1 of Legislative Decree no. 126/1990 in 1993 and 2012. In both cases, the court held that the contested criterion, laid down in art. 3 and applied by the joint committees, was compatible with the Constitution.

---

[4] 'The party with an interest in bringing proceedings shall convene the other party, by communicating in writing its claims and providing the evidence on which it bases those claims. The meeting shall be convened by registered post with a form for acknowledgment of receipt, or by personal delivery of the letter. A period of at least thirty days shall elapse between the date of receipt of the documents and the date fixed for the meeting of the joint committee. The committee shall be made up of three representatives from each denomination. If the committee does not meet within the period established in its mandate, or if the committee does not reach a conclusion or if one of the parties is dissatisfied with the decision taken by the committee, the party with an interest in bringing judicial proceedings may do so under ordinary law. The action shall be examined by the courts. The action shall be exempt from court tax.' (Law no. 182/13 June 2005).

Case of Lupeni Greek Catholic Parish and Others v. Romania

These are the main premises concerning the retrocession of places of worship that belonged to the Greek Catholic Church until 1948. Amongst them the existence of a special law was highlighted, determining the juridical status of these properties. It was against this background that the specific case under consideration was recently judged by the ECHR.[5]

A Greek Catholic parish in Lupeni (Hunedoara County, in central-western Romania) was legally re-established in 1996. In 2001, the parish initiated legal proceedings aiming at the restitution of its ecclesial properties (a church and a plot of land) that had been transferred to the Orthodox Church in 1948. In 2009, the Greek Catholic parish won the case in front of the Court of First Instance (the county tribunal), which judged the case merely on the basis of the titles of ownership, with no regard for Decree no. 126/1990. However, in 2010, the Court of Appeal ruled in favour of the Orthodox community and, a year later, in 2011, the High Court of Cassation and Justice of Romania issued a definitive decision confirming the ruling given by the Court of Appeal, arguing that the desire of the faithful has to be taken into consideration, as provided by the Legislative Decree no. 126/1990, amended by law no. 182/13 June 2005 (see footnote 4).

---

[5] In what follows, we will closely follow the clear and concise presentation of this case on the official website of the ECHR. The quoted paragraphs are written between brackets. GRAND CHAMBER, Case of Lupeni Greek Catholic Parish and Others v. Romania (Application no. 76943/11), Judgment, Strasbourg, 29 November 2016: http://hudoc.echr.coe.int/eng?i=001-169054.

The European Court of Human Rights

Denouncing as unjust the criterion set by the special law in 1990, the complainants brought their case to the ECHR (3rd section). On the one hand, they denounced the violation of their right of access to a court and, on the other hand, the principle of legal certainty, based on art. 6 §1 of the Convention (fair trial within a reasonable timeframe) considering the excessive length of the restitution procedure. Moreover, the applicants invoked art. 13 of the Convention (the right to an effective recourse), as well as art. 14 (against discrimination), arguing that they were discriminated in their access to the court on the basis of their religious affiliation. In their view, the definitive ruling of the High Court of Cassation and Justice violated their religious freedom on the basis of art. 9 of the Convention, whether of itself or in relation to art. 14, as well as their right of ownership on the basis of art. 1 of Protocol no. 1.

In May 2015, the court of seven judges unanimously dismissed their claim, concluding that their right of access to a court and legal security was respected, the Romanian courts having rightly weighed the various interests involved in the case and issued detailed and motivated decisions. However, the length of the procedure was too long. The judges also unanimously held that there had been no violation of art. 14 taken in conjunction with art. 6 §1 of the Convention (§6), and noted that the Constitutional Court had emphasised the need to protect the freedom of religious communities and the freedom of others while having due regard for the historical background of the case.

The applicants then appealed to the Grand Chamber. On this occasion, they raised four complaints (§64), relying on art. 6 §1, 13 and 14 of the Convention, as follows:

- They complained that there had been a breach of their right of access to a court, because the domestic courts had not determined their dispute by applying the rules of ordinary law, but following the criterion laid down by Legislative Decree no. 126/1990, applicable in the context of the non-contentious procedure, namely the wishes of the worshippers in the community in possession of the property.

- Without referring explicitly to the principle of legal certainty, the applicants submitted that the application of this criterion had not been foreseeable and had rendered their access to a court illusory.
- They complained about the length of the proceedings.
- The applicants invoked art. 14 of the Convention, claiming they have been discriminated in their right to access to a court because they belonged to a minority denomination in Romania.

The Grand Chamber chose to examine only the first three complaints and this solely under art. 6 §1, taking the view that the guarantees of art. 13 were absorbed by the stricter guarantees of art. 6.

After a public hearing on 2 March 2016, the Grand Chamber published its decision on 29 November 2016.

As far as the first two claims related to the rights of access to a court, the court ruled that this right was respected and the claimants were not in any way hindered in bringing their case in front of the internal courts (§106-107). As art. 6 of the Convention does not address the application of a certain national law, the 'will of the faithful' criterion cannot be seen as limiting the sovereign right of the court to decide. National courts have full jurisdiction in applying and interpreting national legislation, particularly in cases involving disputes between different religious communities concerning places of worship (§101-102), and the ECHR will not go over the margins of appreciation of Member States on this regard.

However, given the variation that could be seen throughout time in the interpretation of the legislation by various national courts, the ECHR considered that this point should be examined in the light of compliance with *the principle of legal certainty*, and not that of access to a court (§105).

As mentioned, art. 3 §1 of Legislative Decree No. 126/1990 was amended in 2005 in the sense that the party interested in bringing judicial proceedings could do so under ordinary law. The problem arising from this amendment was that this concept of ordinary law became a source of differing interpretations. Some courts had given it the usual meaning of protecting right of ownership and had dealt with actions for recovery of possession in the traditional manner under the Civil Code (i.e. looking at the titles of ownership); others considered that they were required to take into account the wishes of the faithful of the religious community in possession of the property at the time when its legal status was being examined, as foreseen by the Legislative Decree from 1990.[6] Noting that the fluctuations in judicial interpretation from 2007 to 2012 originated in the High Court's case law, the ECHR ruled that 'profound and long-standing differences' existed in the case law (§128) in the present case. Nevertheless, since 2012, the High Court and the Constitutional Court aligned their respective positions and confirmed that the criterion laid down in art. 3 of Legislative Decree no. 126/1990 was to be applied in procedures concerning the restitution of places of worship. The court also noted that, in practice, this has resulted in the harmonisation of the case law of the lower courts. The Grand Chamber concluded that the context in which the action brought by the applicants was examined, namely one of uncertainty in the case law, coupled in the present case with the failure to make prompt use of the mechanism foreseen under domestic law for ensuring consistent practice even within the highest

---

[6] See Frank Cranmer, 'Expropriated church property: Lupeni in the Grand Chamber' in Law & Religion UK, 1 December 2016, on http://www.lawand religionuk.com/2016/12/01/expropriated-church-property-lupeni-in-the-grand-chamber.

court in the country, had undermined the principle of legal certainty and had the effect of depriving the applicants of a fair hearing (§134).

Having extended over a period of almost 10 years, the Court also held that the applicants' case had not been heard within a reasonable time, as required by Article 6 §1.

The fourth claim, under art. 14, corroborated with art. 6 §1 of the Convention, related to the claimants having been discriminated in their right of access to a court because they belonged to a minority denomination. Here, the Grand Chamber did not see a difference in treatment between the applicants. In its view, applying the criterion of the worshippers' wishes had not created a difference in treatment between the Greek Catholic and Orthodox parishes in the exercise of their right of access to a court. Both enjoyed access to domestic courts, which had full jurisdiction to apply and interpret the domestic law and which exercised a review that was sufficiently wide to satisfy the requirements of Article 6 §1 (§172-173). The court also pointed out that this criterion should be considered within the historical and social context of Romania, where the places of worship being reclaimed by the Greek Catholic parishes had been transferred to the Orthodox parishes following the dissolution of the Greek Catholic denomination in 1948. Moreover, when it was enacted in 1990, the legal provision in question had been drawn up after consultation with the interested parties and out of a desire to maintain neutrality, and aimed at respecting the freedom of the former Greek Catholic but now Orthodox worshippers' right to decide on their faith and the fate of places of worship (§170).

Finally, the court held that there had been no violation of art. 6 §1, in respect of the right of access to a court, nor of art. 14, considered together with art. 6 §1, in respect of the applicants' right of access to a court in comparison with the Orthodox parish. Yet, the court recognised that there had been a violation of art. 6 §1 on account of the breach of the principle of legal certainty and of the length of the proceedings.

Conclusion

This paper focused on a case of restitution of places of worship belonging to the Greek Catholic Church in Romania that were then transferred to the patrimony of the Romanian Orthodox Church during the communist regime. This issue concerns a significant number of properties and represents a particularly sensitive social problem.

The ECHR in Strasbourg was called to rule on the implementation of a special law (Decree 126/1990) to determine the juridical status of these properties. The criterion put forth by this law is the 'will of the faithful' of those communities. The Great Chamber ruled that, in this case, the implementation of the will of the faithful principle did not create a discriminatory situation concerning access to the court by the two religious communities. Even though this will of the faithful principle was interpreted differently by Romanian courts from 1990 until 2012, the High Court of Cassation and Justice and the Constitutional Court eventually made it prevail by issuing the definitive ruling.

The Strasbourg-based court will soon have to rule on a few other similar cases concerning the restitution of places of worship. It is, however, obvious that the above-mentioned ruling will determine ECHR jurisprudence. In 2017, two other decisions were published by the court: Glod Greek-Catholic Parish v. Romania and Orăș̦ie Greek Catholic Parish v. Romania. They both follow the same direction as the Lupeni case presented in this paper.

14

CYPRUS

His Grace Bishop Porphyrios of Neapolis, Church of Cyprus

In July 1974, Turkey invaded Cyprus with a large military force, taking advantage of the coup d'état carried out by the military junta in Greece against Archbishop Makarios III, the elected President of the Republic of Cyprus. On 16 August, the fighting stopped but, forty-three years on, the wounds to the body of the island have still not healed. 37% of its territory remains occupied by the Turkish army, which maintains a force of 40,000 soldiers there. In so doing, it has made Cyprus one of the most heavily militarised places in the world. Approximately 180,000 Greek Cypriots were expelled from their homes and properties. Today, around 500 remain enclaved in the Karpas peninsula and the Maronite villages. In November 1983, the occupation regime declared the independence of the so-called 'Turkish Republic of Northern Cyprus', in a move that was condemned by the United Nations Security Council. No country apart from Turkey has recognised the illegal entity.

As a result of the invasion, sacred monuments and archaeological sites of Christian and other faiths were desecrated, looted and destroyed. Everything that adorned the 575 Orthodox churches in the occupied areas was stolen. Close to 20,000 holy icons, wall paintings, mosaics, gospels, sacred vessels, manuscripts, old books, iconostases and, generally speaking, anything that could be stolen for material gain was looted and sold off abroad. The Church of Cyprus, in conjunction with the responsible state authorities (the Law Office, the Police and the Department of

Antiquities), is constantly making intensive efforts to locate and repatriate its stolen cultural heritage. These items have mainly been found, amongst others, in auction houses and art galleries in Central and Western Europe, the UK and the USA.

This brief presentation will refer to the access to and the use of these monuments and holy places in the occupied area of Cyprus, as well as to the situation as regards Muslim monuments under the jurisdiction of the authorities of the Republic of Cyprus.

Free Access

Around fifty Christian churches can be found within the buffer zone (about 3% of the Republic's territory), as well as within several Turkish military areas. With the exception of the Maronite Church of Saint Marina, no one is permitted to approach or access them. After a two-year effort, religious leaders of Cyprus and the Embassy of Sweden have succeeded in obtaining the approval of the Turkish army and the Turkish Cypriot leader, Mr. Mustafa Akinci, to begin restoration and conservation work on the churches of Saint James and Saint George, which are located in the Nicosia buffer zone. The task was undertaken by the bi-communal Technical Committee on Cultural Heritage.

Inside the fenced-off town of Varosha there are fourteen Orthodox churches. No one is allowed in this area, which is entirely under the control of the Turkish army. These looted monuments have been abandoned to weather elements with no upkeep or protection. Varosha is known around the world as a ghost town due to its isolation and dereliction.

Use of Religious Monuments

These religious monuments and holy sites started being used for other purposes and systematically looted straight after the Turkish invasion. Around eighty churches were converted into mosques, a favourite tactic of the Turks from earlier times. The same was done following their first conquest of the island in 1571, when the Catholic cathedrals of Nicosia (Hagia Sophia) and Famagusta (Saint Nicholas) and a number of Orthodox churches were converted into mosques. The same happened to the churches of the Panagia at Lysi, the Virgin Panayia Evangelistria at Karavas, Saint Ambrosios at Ayios Amvrosios, the Archangel Michael at Pano Zodia, Saint Andrew (Apostolos Andreas) at Neapolis, Nicosia - the biggest church in Cyprus before the invasion, of Christ the Saviour at Akanthou, and others. There are instances where the occupying regime built new mosques with Turkish funding but, while the other churches are not being used as mosques, they are not being returned to or maintained by their rightful owners and have, instead, been put to other uses. Despite efforts made through dialogue among the religious leaders, some monuments are still being used as stables. Examples of this are the church of Saint George at Melounda and the Monastery of the Virgin (Panayia Avgadisa) at Milia, Famagusta.

Many churches such as the churches of Saint Luke at Lapithos, of the Virgin (Panayia tou Trachona) in Nicosia and of the Holy Cross at Kythrea have been turned into cultural centres for dance, handicrafts, and other activities.

The Monastery of Saint Anastasia at Lapithos has been converted into an old people's home and the church of Saint Luke in Nicosia has been given to an NGO. Other churches inside Turkish military areas, such as the churches of Saint George at Kythrea and Voni, are being used as army stores.

After being completely looted, many churches were abandoned to the elements. As a result, many are on the verge of collapse today. Such churches include those dedicated to Saint Anastasios at Peristeronapigi and the Archangel Michael at Hartzia, the Monasteries of Saint Paraksevi at Vasileia, Saint George Rigatis at Kyra and Saint Nicholas at Davlo, and many other churches and chapels in towns and villages.

Since 2011, a small number of the 575 churches have been maintained by the bicommunal Technical Committee on Cultural Heritage. There are seven Orthodox churches and the Armenian Metropolis in Nicosia. The main funding for these projects comes from the European Union. The churches include the church of the Virgin at Trachoni and the church of the Archangel Michael at Lefkoniko.

With very few exceptions, the cemeteries in the occupied areas have been vandalised and ruined. Crosses and gravestones have been smashed and, in many instances, the graves have been obliterated, possibly out of revenge or in an attempt to discover hidden treasures.

The holding of religious services in the occupied areas of the island is not permitted without written authorisation from the regime. In the villages of Rizokarpaso, Ayia Triada and Kormakitis, where enclaved Cypriots live, services are permitted in the main churches without written approval. For all the other occupied churches there are strict criteria and a process which is testing the patience and dignity of those asking for permission to conduct services. Since the opening of checkpoints in 2003, refugees have been asking that services be allowed in their parish or village church once a year, usually on the feast day of the patron saint of the church and village.

Over the past three years, due to the extreme policies implemented by the Turkish Cypriot leadership, the number of church services permitted in the occupied areas has fallen. On average, based on data from the Ministry of Foreign Affairs, it appears that about half of the applications are approved and the others are either rejected or receive no response.

In areas of the Republic under government control, there are approximately 100 Muslim monuments. The vast majority are maintained by the Department of Antiquities and District Administration. The majority of Muslims in government-controlled areas are mainly from the Middle East, Egypt, Libya, etc. working in Cyprus. The Turkish Cypriots permanently residing in the government-controlled areas are very few but eight mosques are operating full-time to fulfil their religious needs. Should they so wish, they may pray in the other mosques once they have obtained the key from the responsible authority. Services are held at two mosques in Nicosia, Larnaca and Limassol respectively, as well as at one in Paphos and one at Dali.

The Church of Cyprus is working with the other religious leaders of the island to bring an end to what is an unacceptable situation in an EU member state and to gain total restoration of religious freedom for all the legal residents of Cyprus. Everyone's help and support is necessary and valuable. The European Union declared 2018 as the European Year of Cultural Heritage. The hope is for substantial progress in this long-suffering country still awaiting redemption.

15

FORMER YUGOSLAVIA

Archimandrite Sava Janjić, Serbian Orthodox Church

The Balkan Wars

The Balkan conflicts during the 1990s demonstrated that deliberate destruction of religious and cultural heritage proves to be one of the most deplorable methods of our times in changing political and ethnic landscapes. It has often been perpetrated quite inexcusably in the name of freedom or even religious ideas.

The armed conflict in Kosovo in 1999 was the last in a series of conflicts that marked the tragic breakup of Yugoslavia amid secessionist wars carving new ethnic states in the territory where diverse ethnicities and cultures had coexisted for centuries.

Although incomparable to the Bosnian war (1992-1995), both in terms of casualties and material damage, the Kosovo conflict produced a chronically unstable situation in the Balkans. The ethnic violence and destruction of the Serbian Orthodox heritage continued even after the armed conflict, which was formally ended eighteen years ago by the UNSC Resolution 1244. From the first day, the UN-led mission in Kosovo (UNMIK) failed to prevent systematic attacks and reprisals by Kosovo-Albanian extremists. They targeted not only Orthodox Christian Serbs but also other non-Albanian communities. The end of the conflict in June 1999 was marked by a massive exodus of more than 200,000

Serbs and non-Albanians (according to UNHCR records). Only a few thousand refugees have returned home so far. In the period of the first five years of the so-called peace, between June 1999 and 2004, 150 Serbian Orthodox churches were either destroyed or seriously damaged by Kosovo Albanian extremists. After the war, hundreds of Serbian Orthodox cemeteries were desecrated, with crosses broken into pieces and bones scattered around the tombs. Even the most important Orthodox Christian heritage sites would have been turned into ashes without the protection of the NATO-led Kosovo peace mission (KFOR), which was promptly deployed around major Serb-Orthodox sites soon after the end of conflict. The armed protection of Dečani monastery continues to the present day and has even increased, especially after four armed Kosovo Albanian ISIS-affiliated extremists were arrested near the monastery in January 2016. Although the former Yugoslav regime and Kosovo Albanian rebel leaders bear direct responsibility for horrendous war-time atrocities in Kosovo, after the end of hostilities in June 1999, regrettably, the international figures and organisations responsible for the UNSCR 1244 implementation remained inexcusably passive in stopping the rule of terror by still-armed Kosovo rebels. The freedom won for Kosovo Albanians became a nightmare for tens of thousands of others who lost their homes after the war and had to flee, despite the international presence and the UNSCR 1244 guarantees.

The humanitarian role of the Dečani monastery was publicly recognised by a number of world leaders for providing shelter to both Christian and Muslim refugees during and after the Kosovo war. Nevertheless, as the first UNESCO World heritage site in Kosovo, this monastery was attacked four times with mortar grenades by armed Kosovo Albanian extremists after the end of the 1999 war. In massive riots in 2004, 50,000 Kosovo Albanians rampaged through Kosovo burning thirty-three Serbian Orthodox churches and two medieval Serbian monasteries in just two days, despite the presence of 30,000 strong NATO-led peacekeeping forces, UN police and other international missions. Thousands of mostly elderly Serb residents who had survived the end of the armed conflict were suddenly forced to flee their homes, which disappeared in flames together with their churches. Thanks to the strong insistence of the EU and US diplomats after the riots, the local Kosovo government supported the reconstruction program (2005-2010) led by the Church of England in which, however, only part of the sites destroyed since the war in 1999 was restored. The Kosovo government suspended the reconstruction in 2010 after their decision to prevent further participation of the Serbian Institute for Protection of Cultural Heritage. Regrettably, many Kosovan churches remain in ruins with hardly any prospect of reconstruction.

This presentation refers exclusively to the post-war destruction of the Orthodox Christian heritage in Kosovo in the time of the internationally sponsored peace. Unlike the fragile but functioning peace agreement in Bosnia Herzegovina, where no cultural and religious sites were damaged since the Dayton Peace Agreement in 1995, Kosovo stands as a deplorable example of the most unfortunate post-conflict mismanagement. Kosovo Albanian extremists took advantage of the international presence to irreversibly change the ethnic and cultural landscape of Kosovo and effectively prevent the return of Serb and other refugees, as well as the reconstruction of their holy sites. Shocking scenes of young Kosovo Albanians climbing St. Andrew church in Podujevo during the 2004 riots, the sight of the breaking of the cross on the dome and it being thrown down to the cheering crowd as the church was set on fire, remains a sad reminder of the fragile peace in Kosovo. For Kosovo Albanian youth born after the war and now radicalised by unemployment, the rampant corruption and the lack of economic perspectives, Kosovo Serbs and their holy sites, remain an easy target to direct their anger. There is an increasing support for nationalist parties on the one hand, and the worrisome growth of the Islamist ideology on the other, presenting new threats for the remaining Kosovo Serbs and their holy sites.

For years after the war, the access to many Serbian Orthodox sites in Kosovo was difficult and was possible only under armed NATO escort. Freedom of movement has now improved. Despite western pressure requiring Kosovo institutions to pass a number of laws regulating minority rights in the last years, the laws on religious freedom and cultural heritage protection are still being blocked by radical political groups advocating the idea of an ethnically-clean Albanian Kosovo while they publicly spread their animosity towards our Church. Laws regulating free access to all religious sites and even decisions of the highest Kosovo courts, which protected the Serbian Orthodox Church property rights, are often ignored by local municipal authorities, which remain under the firm control of former warlords and their clans.

Eighteen years after the conflict, the Serbian Orthodox Church in Kosovo still faces occasional incidents, problems with access to all its sites, difficulties in getting permits for the reconstruction of churches, derogatory graffiti and media defamation etc.. It is exposed to attempts to marginalize Church tradition and culture, although all four UNESCO sites in Kosovo are Serbian Orthodox churches. Church identity, history and property rights are often blatantly denied. This is why European organisations must strongly insist on concrete actions, particularly when Kosovo leaders formally pledge commitment to European values and the future in their public statements.

The UNSC Resolution 1244, which is still legally valid, largely failed to efficiently envisage and ensure a peaceful post-war transition. The wartime repression in 1999 was replaced by another repression after the conflict despite the international presence. Some provisions of the UNSCR 1244 have never been implemented at all. Point 6 of Annex 2 of the Resolution mentions deployment of Serbian personnel around the Serbian patrimony sites, which is now hardly possible after eighteen years of chaos, meaning KFOR peacekeepers' presence remains essential for the safety of those sites and its people. Point 7 of the Annex requests the safe return of all refugees, which is being obstructed by Kosovo authorities and tacitly ignored by the international organisations. It is important to mention that Kosovo's independence was unilaterally proclaimed in 2008, despite the UNSCR 1244 principle of respect of Serbian sovereignty (Annex 8, point 8) and, even without a referendum, as a minimum of democratic standards.

The failure to safeguard vulnerable religious and cultural heritage was partially corrected by the UN sponsored Ahtisaari Plan in 2007. Annex 5 requested the establishment of forty special protected zones around the most important Serbian Orthodox monasteries and other provisions for church heritage. But so far, only one part of the Ahtisaari's principles has been transferred into Kosovo legislation. The Implementation Monitoring Council, the role of which is the overview of the Ahtisari's principles, has not met for two years due to the unconstructive position of the Kosovo government towards the Church and its heritage. That is why the Church strongly insists that the long-term and comprehensive protection of the Serbian Orthodox Heritage in Kosovo needs to be regulated, not only by local Kosovo laws, which may be abrogated sometime in the future and mostly fail in practice, but also with more precise international guarantees within the context of the ongoing EU sponsored Belgrade–Priština dialogue. This dialogue is supported by the Serbian Orthodox Church but only in the context of facilitating a better life for all Kosovo communities within the 1244 UNSCR framework and the status neutrality. The Church deeply respects the principled support of the UNSCR 1244 by the Cyprus government and the fraternal assistance of the Church of Cyprus, as it profoundly supports Cyprus in light of the armed occupation of one part of its territory in the last decades.

In conclusion, religious and cultural heritage must never become a hostage or victim of political and secessionist agendas, as it did in the cases of Cyprus and Kosovo Province, and should be treated as a fundamental right of any community to fully preserve its historical and religious tradition despite political realities imposed by force. The Serbian Orthodox Church remains fully committed to these principles and expect the Conference of European Churches to continue monitoring developments in Kosovo-Metohija and to make additional efforts with European governments to prevent further destruction of the Orthodox Christian religious heritage to ensure full respect of human and religious rights for all.

16

SERBIA-KOSOVO
UNSCR 1244/1999

Archimandrite Sava Janjić, Serbian Orthodox Church

Destruction of religious and cultural heritage during the Balkan wars or, more precisely, the ethnically-based wars and insurgencies fought between 1991 and 1999, which brought about the breakup of the former Yugoslavia, is one of the most painful chapters of post-World War II European history. Although the Yugoslav succession wars were fought in profoundly complicated political and social circumstances, their consequences cannot be fully understood without taking into consideration the dramatic ramifications these conflicts had on all ex-Yugoslavia peoples and their cultural and religious heritage. The worst outcome of these wars was the human casualties and the deep wounds that remain in the Balkans. According to independent sources, the number of overall casualties of these hostilities rises to 140,000. The final picture of the former Yugoslavia shows a country which was probably the most diverse in Europe in terms of its ethnic, cultural and religious composition, split into six UN recognised countries and resulted in a highly disputable situation in Kosovo.[1]

In reports on the destruction of cultural and religious heritage in the territories of Croatia, Bosnia and Herzegovina, as well as Kosovo, there is a tendency by some media to refer to the destruction of Croatian,

---

[1] In this article, Kosovo refers to the official UNSCR 1244 designation of the Kosovo-Metohija province of Serbia.

Bosnian or Kosovan heritage, which is in many ways misleading. In the Yugoslav wars, the religious and cultural heritage sites belonging to all ethnic groups suffered together with their communities, including Serbs who had been constitutive people of both the Yugoslav Federal Republics of Croatia and Bosnia-Herzegovina, not to mention the province of Kosovo-Metohija, as the cradle of Serbian history and culture.

In the Croatian war (1991-1995), dozens of Roman Catholic and Orthodox churches were either destroyed or severely damaged. The operations of the Federal Yugoslav Army around Dubrovnik and Western Slavonia (Vukovar) in 1991 left in its wake tremendous heritage damage, which was documented in a number of local and international reports. Although officially fought in an attempt to prevent the secession of Croatia from the Yugoslav federation, the conflict gradually developed into a bloody civil war between the local Croats and the Serbs who, fearing marginalisation, did not want to support Croatian secession from Yugoslavia. The Croatian war ended with a massive Croatian military operation coded 'Storm' in which more than 150,000 Serbs were forced to flee from majority Serb-inhabited parts of Croatia in 1995. Soon after its beginning in 1991, the war in Croatia evolved into a series of brutal reprisals on all sides. Destruction of the religious and cultural heritage was often employed as a means of causing the greatest possible injury to the other side. The Yugoslav army's uncontrolled destruction of heritage and property around Croatia's medieval city of Dubrovnik in 1991 was intended as punitive rather than an attempt by Yugoslav authorities to prevent the secession of Croatia and preserve Dubrovnik in its integral part. The siege of this ancient city remains one of the most notorious symbols of the Yugoslav war tragedy. At the same time, the final and highly controversial Croatian military Storm operation in 1995 was far more of a deliberate and planned ethnic-cleansing of the area inhabited by Serbs than an attempt to reintegrate that part of Croatia. The Orthodox Serb community in Croatia still frequently faces incidents and provocations despite Croatia's accession to the EU in 2013. The present rise of nationalism, coupled with the revival of the World War II rhetoric in Croatia, leaves Serbs feeling unsafe and isolated. Many Serbian Orthodox churches have still not been reconstructed, especially in the Diocese of Slavonia.

The Bosnian war (1992-1995), although similar, was even more complicated, as the Yugoslav Republic was recognised as a rich mosaic of different cultural and religious traditions before the war. Bosnian Orthodox Serbs, Roman Catholic Croats and the Muslim Bosniaks speak comparable languages and are only different in their religious and cultural traditions. The merging of the ethnic and religious identities was undoubtedly one of the main reasons the religious heritage, as a crucial element of ethnic identity, suffered so much in this conflict. It is important to remark that the Yugoslav wars in the 1990s can hardly be accurately assessed without background knowledge of a similar fratricidal assault during World War II. The multi-ethnic and multi-religious Kingdom of Yugoslavia was similarly divided in 1941, with Nazi-puppet states of Croatia and Albania, including Kosovo, directly occupied by the axis powers. These painful memories were often employed as an excuse for squaring accounts in the second disruption of Yugoslavia fifty years later. The Yugoslav secession wars in the 1990s were, in many aspects, a tragic continuation of old animosities with congruent patterns of destruction of holy sites.

In the Bosnian war during the 1990s, the Muslim community suffered casualties and damage in cultural and religious heritage at the hands of both local Serb and armed Croat groups, which were simultaneously involved in fighting one another in an absurd, full-blown war. When local Croats in Mostar blew up the old Ottoman bridge and the Orthodox Serb cathedral, and when Bosnian Serbs destroyed the

National Library in Sarajevo and the Ottoman Ferhadiya mosque in Banja Luka, it demonstrated how even the most iconic examples of the cultural co-existence in Bosnia and Herzegovina could easily be sacrificed in the name of an inherently immoral and godless nationalist agenda. The Serb and Croat leaders in Bosnia in the 1990s often regarded the Islamic religious sites as symbols of Christian suffering from five centuries of Ottoman rule in the Balkans. At the same time, a number of Orthodox and Catholic sites were mercilessly destroyed and desecrated in areas in which Bosnian Muslim forces prevailed, very often by Muslim volunteers from abroad, including Mujahedeen units within the Bosniak army. According to the Andreas report, around 280 Islamic sites and 60 Roman Catholic churches were devastated in this conflict. The Serbian Orthodox Church's official report documented 130 destroyed Orthodox churches. Along with these places of worship, other cultural sites suffered, including libraries, schools, and archives on all sides. Unlike the damaged Orthodox Christian sites in Kosovo, the heritage of all communities in Bosnia and Herzegovina has mostly been repaired or reconstructed. The Dayton Agreement, which concluded the war in Bosnia and Herzegovina, prompted an urgent reassessment of how cultural property could be protected in times of conflict (Annex 8) and led to a more definitive recognition in international humanitarian law, stating that destruction of a people's cultural heritage is an aspect of genocide.

The Kosovo conflict in 1999 developed in a similar pattern as that of Bosnia and Herzegovina. Although officially justified by the Yugoslav-Serbian authorities as an attempt to crush the ethnic Albanian armed rebellion and prevent the secession of its sovereign territory, the conflict evolved into a war of unruly paramilitary groups that committed horrendous crimes and took every opportunity to hurt the other side by destroying either Islamic or Orthodox Christian sites during the 1999 hostilities. Although the majority of wartime destruction occurred in rural areas where predominantly newly built mosques were targeted, some historical mosques in Priština, Peć and Djakovica also suffered the loss of old Ottoman time bazaars and libraries. In total, 155 mosques suffered during the armed conflict in 1999, according to the Human Rights Watch Report of August 1999. With a few exceptions, the destruction of Serbian Orthodox heritage (150 churches and monasteries) began primarily after the end of the Kosovo war and the deployment of the international civil and military mission.

In conclusion, the Yugoslav secession wars, which historically remain the bloodiest armed conflict in Europe since World War II, have shown that religious and cultural heritage can be deliberately targeted whenever there is an attempt to carve out new borders and change cultural and religious landscapes in previously multi-ethnic and multi-religious territories. As explained in Huntington's book 'The Clash of Civilizations' in 1996, the countries intersected by religious and civilizational fault-lines were the first to fall victim in the remaking of the world order that had preserved European and Middle Eastern peace after World War II. Although the Yugoslav wars were not religious wars, the religious traditions were unfairly abused by political leaders and turned into the banners of war. This is a profoundly important lesson to prevent similar future tragedies by the fostering of more cooperation between religious communities, particularly among Christians, more independence from secular authorities and their ideologies and by encouraging expressions of unequivocal condemnation of destruction of religious and cultural heritage, as well as all other acts of violence, either in times of war or peace.

17

SYRIA

His Grace Bishop Armash Nalbandian,
Primate of the Armenian Diocese of Damascus

Christianity in Syria is very ancient. In fact, one of the earliest Christian communities ever to be established after the resurrection of Jesus Christ was in Damascus. During the Byzantine era, Damascus was the city of enlightenment for Christians and many Christians prospered through learning and openness. The fact remains that the Christians of Syria have been living on these lands long before Islam and Muslims came to be there.

Throughout many eras of history, Christians have co-existed fairly peacefully with followers of the other religions of the Middle East (principally Islam and Judaism). Even after the rapid expansion of Islam from the 7th century AD onwards, many Christians chose not to convert to Islam and chose instead to maintain their pre-existing beliefs. As 'People of the Book', Christians in the region are accorded certain rights by theoretical Islamic law (Shari'ah) to practice their religion free from interference or persecution.

In Syria, Islam is not the state religion. The country is secular, which ensures equality for members of other religions. Christians can buy land and build churches. Clerics are exempt from military service and schools provide Christian and Muslim religious instruction. Unlike other Arab countries, Syria represses Muslim fundamentalism. Emigration is a serious problem for the Christian churches as many Christians have left Syria since the 1960s.

In Syria, Christians formed just under 15% of the population (about 1.2 million people) under the 1960 census but no newer census has been taken. Current estimates (for there are no reliable statistics) put them at about 8% to 10% of the population (1,500,000 to 1,700,000), due to lower rates of birth and higher rates of emigration than their Muslim compatriots.

Syrian Christians were never a closed community, nor are they new to this land; rather, they have been indigenous to this land since the birth of Christianity, and shared in building this country with their fellow brothers who chose the Islam faith. Moreover, Christians of Syria could be known for their integrity and honesty. They helped in building this country and have been accepted to the most prestigious positions. There are notes of differences, in view of the political issues, but these were to be solved through real democracy and not through jeopardising Syria's safety and sovereignty.

The situation in Syria is well known. The people live in bad economic circumstances. Families suffer many humane and social problems due to robberies, kidnappings, shelling, killings, unemployment, etc.. The kidnapping of two archbishops of Aleppo, priests, nuns and others, affected the Syrian Christians, for they are messengers of peace and struggling for the good of all humanity.

On the other hand, churches are doing their best by continuing their services, their prayers and the support and comfort of the faithful. Possibilities and donations and fundraisings were organised (and continue to be because support is still needed), to offer humanitarian, medical, educational and financial help and support to the faithful.

Since the beginning of the Syrian crisis, over six years ago, over 200 churches and more than 1800 mosques have suffered damage and destruction. More than ten million Syrians have lost their homes and are now refugees. 40-50% of Syrian Christians have lost their homes.

Today, ISIS and other extremist organisations are abusing the name of Islam. Killing on behalf of Islam and religion, while judging their deaths to be godly, expiating others, imposing Shari'a, categorising others as infidels or irreligious, have all become common practice. Millions of Christians and non-Christians in the Middle East currently suffer from religious extremism, war and religious and ethnic cleansing. Sunnis are killed by Sunnis, Shias are targeted by Islamist fanatics, Christians and Yezidis were expelled from their homes and towns, children have been orphaned, and millions of people are prevented from living peacefully because of fanaticism and terrorism. This is nothing short of 'the new genocide'.

It has repeatedly been stated that history is not even equipped with the right terminology to address these atrocities. With the aspirations of Middle Eastern people to live in peace while prosperity is being shattered, what kind of future awaits these communities? How can young people fulfil their dreams? Will there be any future for them in their own homeland? This cannot be a hopeless situation and a solution to these challenges is a necessity.

Furthermore, the most adequate assurance for Christians to remain in the Middle East is a strong secular government where all citizens are equal and where Christians do not feel that they are treated as second or even third-class citizens. The international community, no matter how sincere they are in their concern for Christians in the Middle East, will not be able to protect them. Migration, on the other hand, is not the solution for Christians. They need to be encouraged to stay in their homeland. Nonetheless, they can only do that when there is a strong secular government that is able to protect all citizens regardless of their religion or ethnicity.

When the new constitution was rewritten, for example, and allowed other political parties to be established and recognised, this constitution clearly stated that Syrians are *one people* without looking into the sect or religion to which they belong. When the issue of the Muslim presidency made Syrian Christians unhappy, it was not seen as a reason to fight. It was accepted and the discussion postponed to a time when their homeland was no longer in crisis.

With regard to the Armenian community in Syria, the following sums up a few statistics. There is no exact survey or statistic on the casualties.

- There have been nearly 200 victims.
- 450 people have been injured.
- 1200 houses have been bombed and partly destroyed.
- 200 homes have been totally destroyed.
- 900 houses have been damaged (broken windows, doors etc.)
- 120 people have been kidnapped (two were killed and six have not returned and there has been no further information)
- 3300 stores and small to big workshops have been damaged and robbed.
- 17 churches have been destroyed (partly) or have burned down or been damaged or desecrated.
- 19 schools have been attacked and partially destroyed, damaged and robbed.
- 8 Armenian cultural centres have been destroyed (*Agumps*)
- 15 Armenian community buildings have been destroyed or damaged (hospitals, orphanages, homes for the elderly, etc).

ANNEX

Invitation

"Holy Sites" refers to different types of locations: places of worship as well as places with a specific historic and cultural meaning for a given religion. In any case, their integrity is crucial: sociologically for religious and/or cultural identities, legally for the free exercise of Freedom of Religion. Because of this double importance of the issue of "Holy Sites", the Conference of European Churches in partnership with the Representation Office of the Church of Cyprus to the European Institutions has the pleasure of inviting you to a conference.

Places of Worship and Holy Sites in Europe and the Middle East: Status and Protection under National and International Law to be Held at the Classic Hotel, Nicosia/Cyprus 8-10 November 2017

The effective and comprehensive protection of "Holy Sites" through legal tools and public policy are key for the development of social cohesion in inclusive, confident and tolerant societies. Reversely, restrictions relating to their use and most specifically their destruction as a means of psychological warfare in armed conflict add to social erosion, fragmentation and displacement. Perceived merely as relating to things rather than to people, places of worship remained a blind spot in international policy making until the barbaric destructions committed by ISIS in Iraq and Syria.

The renewed interest in effective mechanisms of legal protection in this area has also highlighted a certain lack of vision and the need of effective grassroots engagement. The international community needs to develop approaches to more effectively deploy the existing legal tools and good practices relating to the protection of places of worship.

The present event is an opportunity to relate the work of Conference of European Churches to emerging discourses relating security to heritage, which has become a key commitment of the US State Department, the Foreign and Commonwealth Office and a number of other international agencies.

Holy places can be sources of tensions which can affect the peaceful coexistence instead of fostering social plurality and diversity. Thus, the protection of holy sites is a matter of general interest and not only the concern of believers. The international community needs to recognize that there is a particular right to manage holy sites, a right to own them, to gather there for religious purposes, and to perform religious ceremonies. This means that we are speaking about living heritage of holy places.

In recent history, some of CEC member churches face serious problems in getting and maintaining access to holy places. The Conference will explore key challenges relating to the legal protection of places of worship and challenges and opportunities in this area, including:

- Property rights
- Access
- Destruction of places of worship during armed conflict
- Shared and contested places of worship
- Places of worship and cultural heritage protection – challenges and opportunities
- Mixed regimes - regulating places of worship through religious and secular law
- Human Rights and Religious Worship Cultural Heritage
- The conference aims at identifying effective means of engagement with policy makers and will empower churches to produce a much needed agenda for change in this area. It will also identify forms for effective pursuit of the agenda.

Globethics.net Publications

The list below is only a selection of our publications. To view the full collection, please visit our website.

All products are provided free of charge and can be downloaded in PDF form from the Globethics.net library and at www.globethics.net/publications. Bulk print copies can be ordered from publictions@globethics.net at special rates for those from the Global South.
Paid products not provided free of charge are indicated*.
The Editor of the different Series of Globethics.net Publications is Prof. Dr Obiora Ike, Executive Director of Globethics.net in Geneva and Professor of Ethics at the Godfrey Okoye University Enugu/Nigeria.

Contact for manuscripts and suggestions: publications@globethics.net

CEC Series

Win Burton, *The European Vision and the Churches: The Legacy of Marc Lenders*, Globethics.net, 2015, 251pp. ISBN: 978–2–88931–054–8

Laurens Hogebrink, *Europe's Heart and Soul. Jacques Delors' Appeal to the Churches*, 2015, 91pp. ISBN: 978–2–88931–091–3

Elizabeta Kitanovic and Fr Aimilianos Bogiannou (Eds.), *Advancing Freedom of Religion or Belief for All*, 2016, 191pp. ISBN: 978–2–88931–136–1

Peter Pavlovic (ed.) *Beyond Prosperity? European Economic Governance as a Dialogue between Theology, Economics and Politics*, 2017, 147pp. ISBN 978–2–88931–181–1

Elizabeta Kitanovic / Patrick Roger Schnabel (Editors), *Religious Diversity in Europe and the Rights of Religious Minorities*, 2019, 131pp. ISBN 978-2-88931-270-2

Göran Gunner, Pamela Slotte and Elizabeta Kitanović (Eds.), *Human Rights, Religious Freedom and Faces of Faith Human Rights*, 2019, 279pp. ISBN 978-2-88931-321-1

CEC Flash Series

Guy Liagre (ed.), *The New CEC: The Churches' Engagement with a Changing Europe*, 2015, 41pp. ISBN 978–2–88931–072–2

Guy Liagre, *Pensées européennes. De « l'homo nationalis » à une nouvelle citoyenneté*, 2015, 45pp. ISBN : 978–2–88931–073–9

Moral and Ethical Issues in Human Genome Editing. A Statement of the CEC Bioethics Thematic Reference Group, 2019, 85pp. ISBN 978-2-88931-294-8

Global Series

Philip Lee and Dafne Sabanes Plou (eds), *More or Less Equal: How Digital Platforms Can Help Advance Communication Rights*, 2014, 158pp.
ISBN 978–2–88931–009–8

Sanjoy Mukherjee and Christoph Stückelberger (eds.) *Sustainability Ethics. Ecology, Economy, Ethics. International Conference SusCon III, Shillong/India*, 2015, 353pp. ISBN: 978–2–88931–068–5

Amélie Vallotton Preisig / Hermann Rösch / Christoph Stückelberger (eds.) *Ethical Dilemmas in the Information Society. Codes of Ethics for Librarians and Archivists*, 2014, 224pp. ISBN: 978–288931–024–1.

Prospects and Challenges for the Ecumenical Movement in the 21st Century. Insights from the Global Ecumenical Theological Institute, David Field / Jutta Koslowski, 256pp. 2016, ISBN: 978–2–88931–097–5

Christoph Stückelberger, Walter Fust, Obiora Ike (eds.), *Global Ethics for Leadership. Values and Virtues for Life*, 2016, 444pp.
ISBN: 978–2–88931–123–1

Dietrich Werner / Elisabeth Jeglitzka (eds.), *Eco-Theology, Climate Justice and Food Security: Theological Education and Christian Leadership Development*, 316pp. 2016, ISBN 978–2–88931–145–3

Obiora Ike, Andrea Grieder and Ignace Haaz (Eds.), *Poetry and Ethics: Inventing Possibilities in Which We Are Moved to Action and How We Live Together*, 271pp. 2018, ISBN 978–2–88931–242–9

Christoph Stückelberger / Pavan Duggal (Eds.), *Cyber Ethics 4.0: Serving Humanity with Values*, 503pp. 2018, ISBN 978–2–88931–264-1

Texts Series

Principles on Sharing Values across Cultures and Religions, 2012, 20pp. Available in English, French, Spanish, German and Chinese. Other languages in preparation. ISBN: 978–2–940428–09–0

Ethics in Politics. Why it Matters More than Ever and How it Can Make a Difference. A Declaration, 8pp, 2012. Available in English and French. ISBN: 978–2–940428–35–9

Religions for Climate Justice: International Interfaith Statements 2008–2014, 2014, 45pp. Available in English. ISBN 978–2–88931–006–7

Ethics in the Information Society: The Nine 'P's. A Discussion Paper for the WSIS+10 Process 2013–2015, 2013, 32pp. ISBN: 978–2–940428–063–2

Principles on Equality and Inequality for a Sustainable Economy. Endorsed by the Global Ethics Forum 2014 with Results from Ben Africa Conference 2014, 2015, 41pp. ISBN: 978–2–88931–025–8

Water Ethics: Principles and Guidelines, 2019, 41pp. ISBN 978–2–88931-313-6, available in three languages.

Praxis Series

Christoph Stückelberger, *Responsible Leadership Handbook: For Staff and Boards*, 2014, 116pp. ISBN :978-2-88931-019-7 (Available in Russian)

Angèle Kolouchè Biao, Aurélien Atidegla (éds.,) *Proverbes du Bénin. Sagesse éthique appliquée de proverbes africains*, 2015, 132pp. ISBN 978-2-88931-068-5

Elly K. Kansiime, *In the Shadows of Truth: The Polarized Family*, 2017, 172pp. ISBN 978-2-88931-203-0

Christopher Byaruhanga, *Essential Approaches to Christian Religious Education: Learning and Teaching in Uganda*, 2018, 286pp. ISBN: 978-2-88931-235-1

Christoph Stückelberger / William Otiende Ogara / Bright Mawudor, *African Church Assets Handbook*, 2018, 291pp. ISBN: 978-2-88931-252-8

Oscar Brenifier, *Day After Day 365 Aphorisms*, 2019, 395pp. ISBN 978-2-88931-272-6

Christoph Stückelberger, *365 Way-Markers*, 2019, 416pp. ISBN: 978-2-88931-282-5 (available in English and German).

Benoît Girardin / Evelyne Fiechter-Widemann (Eds.), *Blue Ethics: Ethical Perspectives on Sustainable, Fair Water Resources Use and Management*, forthcoming 2019, 265pp. ISBN 978-2-88931-308-2

Philosophy Series

Ignace Haaz, *The Value of Critical Knowledge, Ethics and Education: Philosophical History Bringing Epistemic and Critical Values to Values*, 2019, 234pp. ISBN 978-2-88931-292-4

Ignace Haaz, *Empathy and Indifference: Philosophical Reflections on Schizophrenia*, 2020, 154pp. ISBN 978-2-88931-345-7